It Is Me...

The Breaking of the Generational Curse

*Motivator
Mikkita L Moore*

It Is Me...
The Breaking of the Generational Curse

It Is Me...
The Breaking of the Generational Curse

Copyright © 2020 Mikkita L Moore and Invisible Daughter LLC. All Rights Reserved. No part of this book may be reproduced or transmitted in any form or by any means, electronic or mechanical, including photocopying, recording, or by any information storage or retrieval system except by a reviewer who may quote brief pages in a review to be printed in a magazine or newspaper, without written permission from the author. Unless otherwise stated, all Bible verses were taken from various versions of the Holy Bible.

ISBN: 978-1-7354792-5-5
Imprint: Invisible Daughter, LLC
Printed and bounded in the United States of America.

It Is Me...
The Breaking of the Generational Curse

It Is Me...
The Breaking of the Generational Curse

Thank You!!

It Is Me...
The Breaking of the Generational Curse

It Is Me...
The Breaking of the Generational Curse

Special Thanks & Dedication

Thank all of you for making this book possible

All the Authors: Mikkita L Moore (The Creator), Latonya Willett, Dr Tamika L Johnson, Cynthia S Newell, Shalonda Taylor Earl, Dorothy Inez Fobbs, Dr. Shawna Whitehead-Starks, Morgana Matthews, Dr. Stacy L Henderson and Tamika Marable

Editor: Tiffany Jasper... Thank You for always making sure Invisible Daughter, LLC books are "write".... Thank you for being an amazing friend, and sister on top of being an amazing PERSON!

It Is Me...
The Breaking of the Generational Curse

Graphic Designer: *Shawn Robinson, of 727 Marketing... It's been a pleasure to work with you!!*

This book is dedicated to all the ladies that is or has taken that amazing Journey to Womanhood... This one is for you!

It Is Me...
The Breaking of the Generational Curse

It Is Me...
The Breaking of the Generational Curse

It Is Me...
The Breaking of the Generational Curse

Table of Contents

Chapter One: The Curse was NOT Mine to Break, **Mikkita L. Moore**

Chapter Two: Not Invited, **Cynthia S. Newell**

Chapter Three: Just Another Queen from Around the Way, **Dorothy Inez Fobbs**

Chapter Four: Anger That Was Embedded In My Bones From The Depths Of My Soul, **Dr. Shawna Whitehead Starks**

Chapter Five: Breaking Generational Curses Through Salvation, **Dr. Stacy L. Henderson**

Chapter Six: Free from the Opinion of Others, **Dr. Tamika Johnson**

Chapter Seven: The Restoration of All Things, **Shalonda Danette Taylor-Earl**

Chapter Eight: My Healing Was Connected to My Forgiveness, **Pastor Morgana Matthews**

Chapter Nine: Disrupted by Division, **Tamika Marable**

Chapter Ten: The Breaking of My Family's Generational Curse, **Latonya Willett**

It Is Me...
The Breaking of the Generational Curse

It Is Me...
The Breaking of the Generational Curse

Chapter One

The Curse was NOT mine to Break

Mikkita L. Moore

It Is Me...
The Breaking of the Generational Curse

Mikkita L. Moore, an author, motivational speaker and mother of five, starting at the tender age of 14 from the South Side of Chicago. Mikkita is a retired, master stylist and cosmetology instructor. She has owned two successful hair salons over a period of 13 years and an event-planning company, *Symply Plyzurez Eventz* since 2004. Mikkita is the CEO of Invisible Daughter LLC, which is the publishing company that specializes in Transparency writing, "Getting the Story Out". Mikkita is also the Founder and CEO of *The Art of Transparency, NFP* an organization with a mission to "Heal ONE Person, One City, ONE State, ONE Nation at a time". Although passionate about teaching others about her journey which includes forgiving a father that wasn't, in her opinion, able to be the model man she had desperately needed as a young girl growing into womanhood, she continued to struggle with her inner feelings. Being able to convey these imbedded emotions is also comforting for her. Learning the *Art of Transparency* is equivalent to facing and being fully aware of who she is, her ability to candidly speak from the heart about real life issues and how to conquer life's trials is one of my greatest gifts.

Speaking to participants is a time for meaningful engagement. Time used to encourage, lead and offer real

It Is Me...
The Breaking of the Generational Curse

life situations and results to enable listeners to truly understand and connect with her, not only as the speaker but to have empathy for the topic. One of the results that Mikkita obtains when speaking to audiences is her dynamic ability to ignite an awakening within those who hear her story. It allows them to realize and understand their issue more clearly, that she has been through similar situations and how they, too, can overcome the feelings and possible stagnations from its impact. These processes are all facilitated with audience in mind.

How beneficial it is to have the skill to ignite the path of change. Mikkita's niche is engaging her teen pregnancy and parenting audiences with realistic topics that help identify the issues and the teens' willingness to work towards resolutions. Her books, *The Letter From, the Invisible Daughter* as well as *The Cause and Effect of The Invisible Daughter*, talks about, among other topics, parenting a child that's different from the rest and her doubts of being a good mother. As she speaks candidly about her thoughts of suicide and being in unsafe relationships that included domestic violence; emotional, mental and physical, she creates and implements strategies to be used in the moment to begin healing processes for others. Most gatherings include hands-on activities. There's only room for results; a growth mindset. Mikkita continues to receive multiple invites to speak due this direct approach which call for peace and progress in the lives of others.

Mikkita along with her tour has scheduled and appeared for several presentations and speaking engagements, over the

It Is Me...
The Breaking of the Generational Curse

last 3 years with heightened interest in each state. Moving forward there will be plans to host back-to-school events, expos, workshops and conferences on healing awareness.

www.mikkitamoore.com

info@mikkitamoore.com

It Is Me...
The Breaking of the Generational Curse

The Curse was NOT mine to Break

Breaking the generational curse.... Wow... For me, this started at the age of 37 when I woke up one morning and realized I was sexed up yet *still* lonely.

At a very early age, I began to associate love with abandonment. Why? Well for me it was seemingly simple... If you never knew what something was you wouldn't know that you were missing it. Love didn't look like what others described it as, it didn't look like the TV or the movies. For me, it looked like abandonment.

Let's journey together, I knew at a very early age that I wanted a family, the white picket fence, the husband, the dog, and the 10... yes, TEN kids running around my big beautiful home. However, that was not my reality; my

It Is Me...
The Breaking of the Generational Curse

reality was being raised by a single mother doing everything on her own, then becoming not only a single mother, but a teenage single mother. I was pregnant by the age of 13 years old, mother at 14 years old and a mother of two by the age of 16 years old... And just for the record my pregnancies were not an accident they were intentional. I didn't at that time even care about the single mother part of it.

My father was absent, my older brother was living his life and not thinking about being a big brother to me, my stepbrothers were more absent than my dad and I really didn't have any uncles in my life either. As my mother was raising us on her own, there were no men in and out of the home. All I knew was my mom being the strong Black Independent Woman.

All the boys (grade school and/or church boys) that I would come in contact with either thought I was the ugly

It Is Me...
The Breaking of the Generational Curse

duckling, or they thought I was fast so they would make sexual advances toward me. I guess being "developed" at 10 was a gift and a curse, all at the same time. All I ever wanted was to be truly loved.

I can remember in grade school liking little boys and they would always talk about me to the other boys, saying how ugly I was. Then as a teenager I was in an emotionally abusive relationship because, one, that's what I saw my mother's relationship, and two, he was the only guy that thought I was beautiful. I stayed with him on and off well into my 20's.

So, you ask where the generational curse comes in? My mother's mother was married several times, having eight children by several different men, and although my mother only has two children, both with the same man, she still was never happily married or in good relationships. So much so, that now, she says she doesn't even want to be

It Is Me...
The Breaking of the Generational Curse

bothered with a relationship of any kind. However, me on the other hand, I want a husband, I want a meaningful relationship with my lifelong partner.

Listening to my mother tell me all of my life, "Men ain't worth a thing,", or "Men are only good for one thing", or "Women that make their own money don't need a man for nothing." Hearing this for years results it to become second nature to believe these things. It didn't help that those words were coming from my MOTHER, the person I trust the most. In turn I grew up treating men like they were only good for one or two things…. I either used them for sex or their money. Using men in this way only led to me feeling insecure and lonely. The insecurity started because I would always think about, *"What if they only used me for my sex the way I thought I was using them"*. Or, what if they used me for my money the way that I used them….

It Is Me...
The Breaking of the Generational Curse

As I stated earlier, the men in my life were absent until recent years and even they did not have great relationships. What I saw in their relationships was control, unhappiness, loneliness, bitterness, multiple women at once, and for the most part the women took care of them financially, (not because they didn't have it but because the men required it, yep, a completely different book all together). This is not what I would call love, to me that's still being unloved. So, with all of this, what do I base my analysis on? Everything around me just didn't look or feel right.

I can remember the few times that I thought I knew what love looked and felt like, the relationships ended up being "situationships". The last one being in 2017 ending early 2018; this man came into my life and played friend for a very long time. He was charming, "loyal", loving, and all-around fun person to be around. We dated endlessly (meaning together from the first day until the last day

It Is Me...
The Breaking of the Generational Curse

everyday) for months. I thought he was the one, we were planning our future together with the intentions of being married when he got back on his feet. HA, that was a joke, I helped him through trucking school, I mean why wouldn't I help him, we were going to be together forever, right? WRONG... As soon as he knew he was going to finish trucking school our arguments became relationship ending words, our love making became fewer and further in-between. It was heartbreaking. I couldn't eat, I couldn't sleep, all I wanted to do was cry and ask God, "Why me Lord?"

When I finally stopped crying and opened my ears to listen, I heard the Lord answer the "Why me?" God said that he showed me from day one that this was not the man for me, but I ignored those signs just wanting to finally be loved like I had seen in the movies and on TV. He said to me that the love he has for me will surpass my expectations and I

It Is Me...
The Breaking of the Generational Curse

will not have to beg at all for it. The man for me will give me just what I need when I need it.... BUT I first have to work on ME.

I spent years upon years looking for love. I wanted Mama's love, so I became a Mama at the age of 14 (pregnant at 13), I wanted Daddy's love so badly that I dated anybody that showed me an ounce of attention; rather the attention was positive or negative, I was in need of it. I spent years in an emotionally, mentally and sometimes physically abusive relationship just to feel "*a*" love. Like I have said before, I saw the red flags in my last relationship, but I can also admit that I saw the signs early on in other relationships as well that I ignored, just so that I could *"feel"* loved. The whole time I am with these men, I don't even realize that the love I was looking for could never be achieved from these types of men. They, too, were broken in some ways,

It Is Me...
The Breaking of the Generational Curse

they, too, had unresolved trauma, they, too, had no clue what love looked or felt like.

I realized that we attract who we are, not necessarily what we want. I was attracting broken men because I, too, was broken. I didn't know who I was or my value. I didn't have a clue how to love on me, so I couldn't dare know how to love others. I need not even talk about how I couldn't truly fathom receiving love holistically, when I didn't know how to give love holistically. Hunnni... It is something when you take the mask off and truly see the Generational Curses that you have completely taken on as your own. Please know and understand that this love thing was never *MY Generational Curse to Break... However, This thing Stops with ME!*

Over the last couple years, and I do mean 2 maybe three years, I have really been praying and asking God to change my mind-set towards relationships, love, and friendships.

It Is Me...
The Breaking of the Generational Curse

Change my heart to be open and ready to receive the love that I know I was made to have. I have had to work on my self-worth, my self-image, as well as my thoughts around who and who's I am. I won't say it's been easy to unmask the real Mikkita but I know in the end it will be all worth it.

It takes a lot of courage, humbleness and fearlessness to look yourself in the mirror and truly talk to the little girl inside you. Believe it or not, I am often that little girl that is still waiting on Daddy's approval. I am still that 9-year-old girl who still remembers that the first thing that she heard from her Daddy was, "Hey, 'Black Gal'", not even knowing that I hated that my skin color was so dark.

Loving on me has been the hardest curse to break… There is this saying *"Heal a Woman and you heal every person that comes behind her"*. I never knew what that saying meant until I began to peel the layers of this *"Generational Mask"*: the mask of, I don't need anyone else, the mask of I am strong and independent, the mask of hurt, pain, and childhood trauma. I never knew that I was still hurting from

It Is Me...
The Breaking of the Generational Curse

not being hugged or cuddled as a kid. Standing in the mirror every morning and not even knowing the person I was looking at (or the person who was looking back at me). That is so very impactful.
The Bible says:

Proverbs 19:8, ESV, [8] Whoever gets sense loves his own soul; he who keeps understanding will discover good.

Psalm 139:13-15, ESV, [13] For you formed my inward parts; you knitted me together in my mother's womb. [14] I praise you, for I am fearfully and wonderfully made. Wonderful are your works; my soul knows it very well. [15] My frame was not hidden from you, when I was being made in secret, intricately woven in the depths of the earth.

I read these bible verses faithfully, I give myself daily affirmations and I celebrate the small wins every day. The desire of my heart is to be loved genuinely, whole-heartly, lovingly, and unconditionally. I can no longer worry about the past and allow the past to dictate my future at all. I have to stand on the word of the Lord to heal not only me, but to break this horrible cycle of not knowing what love looks

It Is Me...
The Breaking of the Generational Curse

and feels like. Know every day is not easy but every day is a new day to get it right, to tell myself *I AM ENOUGH*.... Sometimes I wish I was able to go to my mom and have these conversations of growth but unfortunately, she is not open enough to hear that real love is needed, real love is wanted. She has been hurt by love in many ways and to that I am sorry, not sorry because I take on the burden of what others may have done to her but sorry because she deserves to see, feel, and know love on a level like never before. My prayer is that God allows her to at least see me being loved for real before she leaves this earth. I want her to see that it is truly possible and see that love does not have to hurt.

1 Corinthians 13:4-8, ESV, ⁴ Love is patient and kind; love does not envy or boast; it is not arrogant ⁵ or rude. It does not insist on its own way; it is not irritable or resentful; ⁶ it does not rejoice at wrongdoing, but rejoices with the truth. ⁷ Love bears all things, believes all things, hopes all things, endures all things. ⁸ Love never ends. As

It Is Me...
The Breaking of the Generational Curse

for prophecies, they will pass away; as for tongues, they will cease; as for knowledge, it will pass away.

My prayer is that I get to help the generations to come to know that they, too, can heal from the childhood traumas that hinders them. They too can know what real love looks and feels like on the level that they need. I am truly a walking testimony of how loving yourself literally changes your life. It changes how you look at relationships, changes how you look at love and it will also change how you look at your friendships.

Love does not just mean having a partner, but it includes friends as well. When you do not know how to love, what it is or what it feels like, you can't deal with real friendships well. But that subject is an entirely different book. Understanding and how to cultivate friendships and how to be a friend is definitely topics that I had to learn.

It Is Me...
The Breaking of the Generational Curse

In closing, I want you to know that I am a work in progress on this journey to break this generational curse. However, I can tell you that I am so far from where I was a couple years ago, which is proof, I am growing for the better (or an ending similar to this).

Deuteronomy 31:6, ESV, ⁶ Be strong and courageous. Do not fear or be in dread of them, for it is the Lord your God who goes with you. He will not leave you or forsake you."

It Is Me...
The Breaking of the Generational Curse

It Is Me...
The Breaking of the Generational Curse

Chapter Two

Not Invited

Cynthia S. Newell

It Is Me...
The Breaking of the Generational Curse

Cynthia S. Newell is the owner of Cynthia Sherrell Enterprises and Dare to Dream where she is affectionately known as the R.I.S.E & W.I.N coach.

Through her wisdom and guidance, she coaches women visionaries & support them with giving voice to their vision so that it has FULL expression in their life.

As a speaker, mentor, motivator and author Cynthia's heartfelt intention is to encourage and empower through inspirational teaching, spiritual enlightenment, and guided transformation.

On her down to earth podcast, *"From Powerless to Powerful"*, listeners laugh & learn from personal experiences that strengthened her faith & gave her wisdom on how to move from a place of powerlessness to powerfulness.

Her Facebook broadcast, *"R.I.S.E & W.I.N Tips"* supports hundreds with releasing internal struggles effortlessly & walking in newness. Clients enrolled in her *R.I.S.E & W.I.N Group Coaching* program learn to clarify their vision, stop feeling lost and being last in their life and create a life they love waking up to.

For nearly 20 years Cynthia's has learned to use her dreams to resolve inner conflict, identify motives, and embrace a fuller identity. She now teaches dream interpretation and

It Is Me...
The Breaking of the Generational Curse

uses her prophetic gift to support others with pinpointing patterns, recurring themes and identifying God messages in their dreams.

Her e-book, *"Dreams Speak: Getting the Most Out of Your Dreams"* provides spiritual support on remembering dreams, understanding dream messages, decoding symbolism & seeing where the message applies in one's waking life.

Learn more about Cynthia at www.cynthiasnewell.com

It Is Me...
The Breaking of the Generational Curse

NOT Invited

A woman's wedding day is one of the most special days of her life. When my middle daughter told me that she was getting married, I was elated! Like most mothers, I had envisioned an extravagant ceremony with my oldest daughter being the maid of honor and my youngest daughter being a junior bridesmaid. I daydreamed about how proud I would be to see all three of my girls looking radiant and celebrating together. The joy of seeing my girls' bond with one another through tears, laughter and hugs made my heart skip a beat. I was ready to gleam with delight and praise God for the perfect day I knew it was going to be.

My lovely vision was brought to a screeching halt when my daughter decided that her sisters were not invited to her wedding.

It Is Me...
The Breaking of the Generational Curse

I was furious, livid to be exact.

Who wouldn't want their sisters at their wedding? My daughter stated that she wanted an intimate wedding with only parents. I tried to be okay with her decision but I wasn't. I wanted her to see the long-term affect her decision would have on her relationship with her sisters. She could not understand why her sisters were upset and did not back down on her decision. I kept praying that she would change her mind because I could see how this decision was feeding into the pathology of broken sister relationships that had plagued our family for generations. One Saturday morning my oldest daughter called to talk to me about not being invited to the wedding. Through her tears she said, "We've been through so much together, why wouldn't she want to share this beautiful moment with me?" I understood her pain and her sadness. When I asked

It Is Me...
The Breaking of the Generational Curse

if she had spoken to her sister about her feelings she said yes but her sister did not change her mind.

I could tell that the situation started to bother my soon-to-be-married daughter when she randomly stopped by my house. She could not understand what the big deal was and why her big sister was so upset especially since she was aware of this decision for some time. As carefully as I could, I explained to her that people who love you want to be a part of the special moments in your life and want to share in your joy.

My daughters decided to stop speaking to one another. Growing up, when they would have a disagreement or fight, I tried to teach them how to be rational and how to talk things out so that the problem could be resolved and not linger and fester into something bigger. It was important to me that my daughters understood the value and necessity of sharing a relationship with each other.

It Is Me...
The Breaking of the Generational Curse

Knowing how to resolve conflict, forgive and establish boundaries was essential. I get it, sisters disagree and may not speak to each other for a few days, but to go months or years without speaking was absurd. It was important to me that my daughters did not behave this way.

The bond of sisterhood creates security and boost confidence. Sisters are one another's first best friend. Sisters keep each other's secrets. It's your sister that is usually the first person we tell about our first crush. Sisters give each other fashion advice, protect each other and listen to the matters of the heart without judgment. It is through sisterhood some women learn how to be selfless, how to communicate and how to be emotionally available for someone else. The relationship between siblings is the baseline to every relationship that follows it.

It Is Me...
The Breaking of the Generational Curse

For my entire life, I've watched the relationship between my mom and aunts. There has always been disconnection and a lack of consistent closeness between them. Though they had many similarities – motherhood, workforce, and romantic relationships – a steady sisterhood bond was not one. Occasionally, there were temporary moments of closeness, but it was short lived and replaced with contempt, disassociation and separation. Division has plagued my family and has stolen the gift of togetherness, the promise of family security and the hope of trusted relationships.

In most cases, my mom and her sisters pulled together in times of crisis to get things done so they could move on but not to support each other or to talk about their feelings. The day my grandmother passed away, the sisters never embraced each other, or cried in each other's arms, instead,

It Is Me...
The Breaking of the Generational Curse

each found things to do to clear out my grandmother's belongings as her lifeless body lay in the nursing home bed. The one year anniversary of my grandfather's death was painful for all of us. My mom stayed in bed practically all day. My aunt literally cried all day. Everyone seemed to be in a fog. After consoling my mom and aunt, I suggested that the two of them do something together. I felt it would be nice for them to bond through this experience. When my aunt texted my mom, my mom was not very welcoming she suspicious about why my aunt was texting her. My aunt called my mom but she missed the call, when my mom called my aunt back, my aunt didn't answer. It was disheartening to see her avoid my aunt; it was even sadder that she denied herself the opportunity to connect and to be supported through her own grief.

Sometimes having a close sister relationship is simply not possible. It's been a little over a year since my sister and I

It Is Me...
The Breaking of the Generational Curse

have spoken. For years I have tried to keep our relationship on solid ground by dismissing her inability to be there for me when I needed her and intentionally overlooking her selfishness. Having a relationship with my sister was important, so I often chose to forgive her for the times she would disrespect and dishonor me.

When her marriage ended, she was distraught. I would talk to her for hours to help her cope and sort through her thoughts and feelings; I believed that's what good sisters do. When I found myself in the same situation a year later, I was not able to be the sister she was used to me being. My life was shattered and I was devastated. I assumed that my sister would understand some of what I was feeling since she had recently gone through it herself, but she seemed oblivious. When she needed to vent and complain about her life, I couldn't be there for her. When she wanted to talk bad about her ex-wife and blame the world for her

It Is Me...
The Breaking of the Generational Curse

life, I couldn't be there for her. My sister became so angry; she said some very hurtful things before pushing me out of her life.

I chose not to push my way back into my sister's life. The rage and fury she spewed hurt me deeply because it was not that I was intentionally trying not to be there for her, I just needed to be there for myself. I was an emotional wreck and did not have the energy or mental space to take on her issues. I needed myself so that I could process where I was in my life, how I got there and where I was headed next. I decided to steer clear of the relationship so that I could focus on my mental and emotional well-being.

While it may appear that I and my sister's relationship is following the same pathology that has plagued my family for decades, it is not. Some things have to be broken down to nothing so that it can be rebuilt into something beautiful. Relationships require standards, boundaries and respect.

It Is Me...
The Breaking of the Generational Curse

These things were never established in our relationship, they were instituted by default. The years of me accepting our lopsided relationship and not speaking up about it made her think that I approved her behavior. Not calling her out on her volatile behavior or making excuses for the many emotional outbursts made her think it was okay to behave that way.

I know in my heart that my sister and I will share another relationship; however, the relationship will be a mutually beneficial relationship. In a recent dream my sister came over to my house to visit our mother. Though we were not speaking she had keys to my new car, a white Dodge charger. As I am parking my other car, my sister quickly hops out of her car and rushes over to my new car and gets into the driver seat. She didn't acknowledge my presence or ask my permission to get into my car before starting the

It Is Me...
The Breaking of the Generational Curse

engine. I felt disregarded, dismissed and disrespected by her actions.

This dream spoke volumes. It came to make me aware of the fact that when my sister and I enter into our new relationship (white car represents rebirth) that clear boundaries must be established immediately. Her having keys to my new car was indicating that she still has access to my life however her actions demonstrated that if I do not actively and honestly make clear to her what I will and will not tolerate, I will feel disregarded, dismissed and disrespected in the relationship.

The pathology of broken sister relationships stops with me because I am willing to be the voice of reason regarding issues that come up between my daughters. I am willing to take the time to talk through issues and challenges rather than ignore them. I am willing to listen with an unbiased heart and respect views that are different than mine. I am

It Is Me...
The Breaking of the Generational Curse

willing to speak the truth in love and pray fervently about things that are out of my control.

This generational curse stops with me because I have taken the scripture, Titus 2:3-5 as my life's intention, "Likewise teach the older women to be reverent in the way they live, not to be slanderers or addicted to much wine, but to teach what is good. [4] Then they can urge the younger women to love their husbands and children, [5] to be self-controlled and pure, to be busy at home, to be kind, and to be subject to their husbands, so that no one will malign the Word of God."

My middle daughter married the love of her life on April 3, 2021, with her big sister right beside her. As a mom, I was proud that both of my daughters took my advice to pray about the situation. I was grateful to God for answering my prayer and helping my daughter to see the value in having her sister take part in her special day. I couldn't stop

It Is Me...
The Breaking of the Generational Curse

smiling. I praised God for touching both of my daughters' heart. I praised God for allowing my oldest daughter to forgive her sister for unintentionally hurting and for deciding to come to the wedding. I praised God for dismantling a generational curse that has plagued my family for decades.

A sister's love strengthens and encourages one's heart; from it you can soar high and overcome any challenge. Sometimes a sister's love may feel distant and distorted, in those moments, offer prayer and patience to your sister and to the relationship. No matter how strained the relationship becomes with your sister, have faith and move in love. "Love is patient and kind; love does not envy or boast; it is not arrogant or rude. It does not insist on its own way; it is not irritable or resentful; it does not rejoice at wrongdoing, but rejoices with the truth. Love bears all things, believes

It Is Me...
The Breaking of the Generational Curse

all things, hopes all things, and endures all things. Love never ends." I Cor. 13:4-8

It Is Me...
The Breaking of the Generational Curse

Chapter Three

Just Another Queen from Around the Way

Dorothy Inez Fobbs

It Is Me...
The Breaking of the Generational Curse

Dorothy Inez Fobbs

(A.K.A. Phenom D.I.V.A) a 50-year-old African American Queen who hails from "Around The Way" in Decatur Illinois.

She notes that she has always been known to have a lot to say. She has always been a go getter with big dreams of being famous in some type of way. Growing up she loved music and dancing. She always thought that she would do some work in the Entertainment Industry. She has a big heart of GOLD. She has always loved helping and being there for others. Even the stray cats weren't safe from being saved by her as a child. She has multiple degrees in the Social Services field, and She has served in the field working multiple jobs for about 20 years.

Today, she stands before us as a woman who has had many trials and tribulations that have all turned into triumphs. It was about 15 years ago when she was forced for to make some major life changes after a 15-year relationship with the father of her children ended. She moved from Illinois to Virginia in 30 days post the break up. She moved solo temporarily without her children, with a U-Haul full of clothes, and a used car that she had just bought. She verbalized that life happened for real. She stated that it was either sink or swim. She quotes that she chose to fly!!!!! With no regrets she decided to see her circumstances as a blessing that needed to happen. She states that through her trails she found the true Queen that she was destined to be.

It Is Me...
The Breaking of the Generational Curse

Her life and journey continue as she has recently moved to Georgia to expand and network as a Professional Life Coach. She states that her goal in life is to be free and to move to the beat of her own drum!!!!

It Is Me...
The Breaking of the Generational Curse

Just Another Queen from Around the Way

Sisterhood......Am I My Sister's Keeper....... Really?

This is a phrase most of us may know well. It sounds good, and it has been a trending phrase among African-American Women and other empowerment type groups and organizations. This phrase became the hardest lesson that I had to learn, and unfortunately it became the source of the trauma that I experienced. Who would think that there could be trauma in this? Here is where I discuss a lesson in breaking the generational curse.

Trauma

When I think of the trauma that I have experienced, I have come to realize that everyone experiences trauma differently. Trauma can be described as a deep disturbing experience. Most people will place trauma in the context

It Is Me...
The Breaking of the Generational Curse

of being the unthinkable or a horrific or even a tragic incident that deems to not only be life changing, but the experience can cause lifelong effects that may hinder an individual's everyday experiences with life in general. I can't place my trauma in that context, but I can place my trauma in the context of being more Emotional/Psychological.

Emotional/Psychological Trauma can be defined as being the result of extraordinarily stressful events that shatter your sense of security while making a person feel helpless. Psychological trauma can make it difficult for an individual to handle or deal with upsetting emotions and memories. These emotions and memories can show up as recurring triggers that may cause an individual to experience some form of anxiety. The anxiety will then cause an individual to feel or become disconnected, and they may ultimately find it difficult to trust others. This is exactly what I started

It Is Me...
The Breaking of the Generational Curse

to experience, but I didn't necessarily identify what I experienced as TRAUMA.

Who am I?

All I ever wanted to do was to…. Just …Be… Me… There was a day when I really didn't believe that there was anything different about me. Everyone is different or unique in their own way. For me I would say that it starts with my name. When I say different, I am speaking of the meaning and circumstances behind the very name I was given. I didn't make a connection to these facts until recently. I am….. Dorothy Inez Fobbs……. I was named after my father's mother, Dorothy, and my mother's mother, Inez. This was definitely different because the name Dorothy wasn't very common among my age group. I can admit that I had a hard time embracing my name growing up. My middle name, Inez, was just different. I thought I was the only other person besides my

It Is Me...
The Breaking of the Generational Curse

grandmother who had that name. So, what's in a name? I remember when I was curious about the meaning of the name that I was given at birth. This inquiry came at a time in my life when I was beginning to look for a deeper meaning in life. My first name, Dorothy, carries the meaning of .... God's Gift, or A Gift of God. Gift speaks of "Spiritual Gift or Gifts. My middle name, Inez. has the meaning of.... Holy...Pure.... Chaste. When I was able to process and resonate with the meaning of my name, I was able to embrace and use my full name with a sense of pride. This totally explains the story of who I am and how I came to be.

I was born in Decatur, Illinois. Decatur is a small industrial town with a lot of history and heart. I am the daughter of Annie Marie. She was a very strong and loving mother who taught me to fight from the time I took my first breath. We almost didn't make it. She had me when she was 36. I

It Is Me...
The Breaking of the Generational Curse

was called a Miracle Child that came after 5 miscarriages. My mother was a very caring woman who worked as a CNA for over 30 years. She taught me how to have compassion for others. I watched as she participated in the community with the Elks Club. I am also the granddaughter of Dorothy and Inez. My grandmother Dorothy was a strong and very religious woman who dedicated her time in church, and she also mentored young women. I guess that is where I got that from. Inez was a passionate southern woman. She was a farmer and homemaker in Mississippi. I think she was the one that taught me how to cuss. I loved going to the south as a young girl. I loved learning to shell crowder peas and wash greens. I am also the GREAT granddaughter of Estelle Gill. She was G Ma Dorothy's mother and she lived to be 102. Grandma Gill was the mother of her church. I never heard her say much but you could feel the strength and wisdom around her. My

It Is Me...
The Breaking of the Generational Curse

grandmother Dorothy and her siblings always took good care of her. She lived across the street from my grandmother Dorothy. I also have my big Sisters Gail and Carla and a list of aunts and big cousins that taught me how to be the DIVA and DOPE woman I am today. I work so hard because I have some pretty big shoes to fill. I hope I am doing them justice by carrying on our family LEGACY. I AM....DOROTHY INEZ FOBBS.

I was raised to be who I am, and I was raised to believe that I was unique and special. I would say that I grew up pretty normal. I got a chance to enjoy my childhood. I may have been slightly sheltered because I was the baby of the family. I was always treated like that miracle child that I spoke of earlier. I was spoiled rotten according to my sisters. I was kind of shy, but I never had trouble making friends. I was outgoing and athletic. I have always loved music, and I loved to dance. I have always been very

It Is Me...
The Breaking of the Generational Curse

stylish and unique. I have always had a love for fashion. I had no issues getting along with others for the most part. I have always been very observant, and incredibly wise beyond my years. I spent 36 years of my life in Decatur, Illinois. I had my children at the ages of 23 and 29. I enjoyed young adulthood and I had my crew of BFF's that are still a part of my life today. Oh.... if the highways, byways, and clubs could talk. We tore the roads and people's cars up partying like rock stars.

At this point in my life, I thought I knew who I was until I reached the ending of my fifteen-year relationship with the father of my children. No regrets, I learned that no matter how bad you want a relationship to work, people just grow apart. Life goes on. I was heartbroken and looking for a new start, so I moved to Portsmouth, Virginia with family. Let me tell you how Portsmouth, Virginia was like a whole new world. I had never been more than a 10- or 12-hour

It Is Me...
The Breaking of the Generational Curse

drive from home. I moved across the country to start a new life. It wasn't long before I decided to further my career in the social services field by enrolling in graduate school. I obtained two master's degrees, and I was ready to conquer corporate America. I thought moving to a more urban area would be a plus as an African-American woman. Little did I know, how hard it would be for me, mainly at the hands of people that looked like me. It seemed like the more I tried to advance and find better employment, the more I was faced with how I looked to other black women in the workforce. I didn't know what to wear to interviews. My curvy body seemed to be more important than my skill set or my ability to perform on the job. I was constantly faced with issues that really didn't have anything to do with the work. I called this the ……. STRONG BLACK WOMAN THING…. I didn't even realize how affected I was from some of the sore treatment.

It Is Me...
The Breaking of the Generational Curse

Being Me

I recall two incidents that sent me to another place. The first one took place when I was in my first master's program. I was enrolled in a school counselor program. I had an assignment where I had to interview a school counselor from all three grade levels. I went to conduct an interview with an elementary school counselor at a school located in Portsmouth. I check in with the main office and a male school counselor came to escort me to his office for the interview. Not even five minutes into the interview, he received a call from the main office. It was the principal. She inquired about who I was, and what I wanted. The look on the school counselor's face said it all. The principal asked him to bring me back to the main office so she could see me. We complied. The principal tried to act as if she was being nice, but it really didn't come off that way. She wanted to ask me exactly what I planned on

It Is Me...
The Breaking of the Generational Curse

doing with the interview. After feeling interrogated, we walked back to the school counselor's office to continue the interview. Well, let me tell you how the interview turned into a lesson. The male counselor apologized for the principal's behavior, and then he went on to tell me how I would never get very far in the field because of the way that I looked. He told me that he thought I was somebody famous coming to see him. I told you before, "I love fashion". I remember wearing a sweater dress with a turtleneck and boots. I was totally covered up and nothing was skintight. I kept my nails done with designs and my nail have always been rather long. I told you that I was different. The school counselor went on to tell me how other women would constantly be jealous of the way that I looked in a school setting. Although his analogy was defeating, I thought he was crazy. He ended by telling me that he was instructed to keep me in his office. He was told

It Is Me...
The Breaking of the Generational Curse

that he could not give me a tour of the school, and he was told to ESPECIALLY keep me away from the sixth-grade boys classroom. I could not believe it. I was so hurt. The second incident happened when I had an interview at a social services agency where one of my homegirls referred me. She was a supervisor, but she wasn't the person who interviewed me. I thought the interview went well for the most part. I was interviewed by a younger Caucasian lady who really looked like she rolled out of the bed with a hangover. Her clothes were wrinkled, and she had red and purple streaks in her hair. I remember her asking me where I saw myself in the next five to ten years. Awesome question, and I was eager to discuss my dreams and goals. I remember telling her that I wanted to be a life coach and I spoke about some of the stigma connected to mental health. This was during a time when the self-help industry was starting to grow. There were two parts to the interview.

It Is Me...
The Breaking of the Generational Curse

There was the verbal interview and there was also a written portion. I never made it to the written portion. Instead, the lady took me on a tour of offices to supposedly meet some of the administrative staff and supervisors. When I left, I got a call from my homegirl. She asked me what happened. She was wondering why I didn't take the written portion of the interview. I told her I wasn't given a written portion. After she conducted her own investigation, she told me that the lady paraded me around to get an opinion on my outfit. I remember wearing a blouse with ruffles that covered my back side with a vintage vest with vintage buttons on it. I had on dress pants that fit but were not too tight and I had on calf length boots. My homegirl saw me before the interview. I was totally appropriate. Long story short, the girl said I was vague and that she didn't like what I was wearing to the interview. Funny thing is, I was hired there years later. I learned that it was simply the culture of how

It Is Me...
The Breaking of the Generational Curse

they ran their office. Let us just say that it didn't work out because they could not place me in a box. They passed me around to every supervisor they had except my friend, in hopes to somehow "whip me into shape." That didn't work so, yet again, I was faced with rejection for just being me.

Breaking the Curse

Years passed and honestly the same treatment followed me from place to place. I started to believe it had to be me. I grew bitter and ready for whatever, just as a means to protect myself and my dignity while working in the field. This continuous treatment helped shape how I decided to deal with other black women. I wanted no parts of any sisterhood, and I was satisfied with having my real friends back home in Decatur. I gave up on certain jobs, and I only took jobs with male bosses and jobs working in the field. The office was not for me. Although I had received my second Master's in Professional Counseling, I had no desire

It Is Me...
The Breaking of the Generational Curse

to work in the traditional setting. I was told that I didn't look like a counselor, and I was not trying to. I was continuously fighting just to be me. I was going to look and act like me at all costs. I guess that was my way of rebelling against the system. I have never wanted to be like everyone else.

Although I was proud to stand up to being my authentic self, I still didn't realize how any of this treatment affected me until I decided to pursue my life coach career. In the mist of branding myself on social media, I kind of took a detour, and I started engaging into New Edition Fan groups. I started to engage heavily after I completed a program with a professional life coach for myself. She suggested that I engage and embrace other women. I quickly became a highly active fan. I started different groups and I started facilitating several Facebook pages. Along the way I was triggered by what we call internet

It Is Me...
The Breaking of the Generational Curse

trolls. I started to get some of the same behavior that I received in the workforce. I experienced so much hate and disrespect, but I also dished my share of disrespect in return with a vengeance. Then one day I realized how counter-productive this behavior and engagement was for me. I began to grow and change to the point where I was tired of fighting to prove myself, but I was mostly tired of fighting with my sisters. While I was in the middle of my journey for self-love, I realized that the same women that I fought against experienced the same trials and issues of life that I had overcome.

I had been on my journey as a life coach for a few years. I had written a program that never seemed to be finished until I decided to turn my pain into my passion. I decided to make it my mission towards embracing other women instead of continuing to fight and be at odds with them. Here is where I broke the generational curse. I decided to

It Is Me...
The Breaking of the Generational Curse

be......MY SISTER'S KEEPER.... for real. Life is now a journey of peace and happiness. I want to continue to be a leader and teach other women how to be in a place of peace and happiness by embracing one another while learning to love themselves. So far this has been working for me. I feel like this was the best decision for change that I have ever made in my life. There is definitely more to come. Allow me to leave you with this......What other people think of you is none of your business, but most of the time it is a deflection of how they really feel about themselves. Once I learned that....... the world opened up and the curse was forever broken.

It Is Me...
The Breaking of the Generational Curse

It Is Me...
The Breaking of the Generational Curse

Chapter Four

Anger That Was Embedded in My Bones from The Depths of My Soul

Dr. Shawna Whitehead - Starks

It Is Me...
The Breaking of the Generational Curse

Dr. Shawna Whitehead-Starks is a Minister, Evangelists, a Successful Business Women for eight different business here in the State of Wisconsin and is the NAACP Economic Committee Chair for the State of Wisconsin. She is a Founder, CEO, Author, Business Consultant and Business Coach and Motivational Speaker and Seminar Facilitator and speaker, who travels all over the World.

Dr. Shawna Whitehead Starks majored in Islamic Studies from the University of Chicago School of Divinity obtaining her Ph.D. in June of 2020. Dr. Shawna Whitehead Starks was featured in the Shepherd Express in November 2019 as Hero of the Week. I received several awards for Outstanding Leadership and The Future Successful Entrepreneurial Awards.

As of April, 2020 Dr. Shawna Whitehead- Starks, and Co-Founder Sondaya Weddle have written a book together. A Successful Way To Entrepreneurship and Obtaining Wealth. This has been become a #1 seller, throughout the United States. We have many colleges such as Iowa University, Arizona State University, and many entrepreneurial programs have bought their book to help facilitate programs within their institutions. The booklet continues to fly off our shelves as more people hear of it.

It Is Me...
The Breaking of the Generational Curse

In the June 2020 Victorious Women Magazine has featured and congratulated Dr. Shawna Whitehead Starks and daughter Sondaya Weddle as Founders and Co- Founders of 8 new businesses.

Dr. Shawna Whitehead Starks Owns and run her very own Podcast Gospel Radio. Walking In Your Destiny Christian Talk Show and WIYD Studios and Internet Radio. Dr. Shawna have been on many radio as well as podcast shows helping others to understand the importance of being or becoming an entrepreneur and obtaining wealth without being in debt, while walking in their purpose.

It Is Me...
The Breaking of the Generational Curse

Anger That Was Embedded in My Bones from The Depths of My Soul

Anger is real and it is a generational curse that I did not purchase, but have carried for so many years thinking that this is who I am. The definition of anger is feeling or showing strong annoyance, displeasure, or hostility; full of anger.

Growing up in a Christian household as a Jamaican woman, raising your voice and having a lot of hostility is how I grew up. My dad is from Kingston, Jamaica and my mother is from Milwaukee, WI. My mother had a gentle and soft-spoken voice and a sweet spirit about her versus my dad who was loving but very hostile and would go from zero to a 100 within a matter of seconds. My dad was a great

It Is Me...
The Breaking of the Generational Curse

family man who did not mess around when it came to his family. My dad loved his family, and would protect his family by any means necessary. My grandfather and great grandfather all suffered from rage and anger. They had no problem pulling out a machete or a gun and would use it. Due to always being around war and violence in Kingston, Jamaica, it became normal behavior. The women in our family had to stay in their place. Their voice did not matter, and the women in my family had to obey their husband if they were married.

My mother was so much different from my dad, due to her being born and raised in the United States, and not being Jamaican, my parents came from different backgrounds. My dad moved to the states four months before my parents married. My dad firmly let my mom know that once they married there is no divorce because my dad does not believe in divorce and neither does my grandparents. God

It Is Me...
The Breaking of the Generational Curse

has given my mother the strength and endurance to deal with my dad's bad temper and anger issues without allowing it to change her.

God has blessed my parents, and they have been married now for 53 years.

I was determined that when I grew up, I would be married, have a family and live happily ever after. In hopes that I would be able to talk to my husband in any way and he will obey me, never cheat on me or leave me. I would pick and choose if I would listen to him because I did not want to ever be treated like or talked to the way the men in my family talked to treated the women in my family. My dad raised me and my sister to be strong, independent, and not to take mess from anyone. Let your voice be heard and don't back down for anyone. I carried that mentality all of my life and did not care who did not like it. I knew that I

It Is Me...
The Breaking of the Generational Curse

could fight, and I was a brown belt in karate and was not scared of anything or anyone.

When I got married to my first husband, I carried all of that anger into my marriage. My husband was 9 years older than I was, and because of it, he would try to talk at me, and treat me like I was a child, even though I was a grown woman. When he would do that, I would curse him out and go off, to the point I would see black. It could be something so small, and I would blow it up to something so big that it would make me break things in our home, and punch holes in the wall. I did not know what was happening to me; all I knew is what I learned when I was younger. My daddy said, "Don't you let anyone talk to you or treat you like you are less than." Every time I would go off or snap and I mean really lose my temper, I would feel so bad after everything was over, and had calmed down. I did not know how to stop my raging anger and bad attitude.

It Is Me...
The Breaking of the Generational Curse

Seeing that type of behavior all of my life, I thought that was normal. Even if I did not pull a gun out on you I would have had you beaten up or jumped. You name it and my family was dealing with you. Allowing myself to get so angry that I would sometimes visually blackout, doing this all in the name of Jesus, claiming to be a born-again Christian and walking in deliverance, while always trying to justify my behavior, and blaming everyone else for my lack of self-control. Not looking at myself while understanding that one day I will have to answer to God for all of my actions and behaviors. God said in his Word that "He will keep you if you want to be kept".

God loves us so much that he continues to show us his grace and mercy. Even in my mess God kept me. When I found out that my husband was cheating on me, I stabbed him and tried to kill him, which I'm not proud of; by His grace, he never pressed charges. I had a rage that I had

It Is Me...
The Breaking of the Generational Curse

never felt in life, and for some reason, God still had his hand of protection on me. My husband asked me to forgive him, and I said I did, but in my heart and mind, I did not. I was angry and was determined to make him pay by getting him back for the hurt and pain he caused me.

I tried to pray about it but instead, I told the Lord, "I got this I'm going to take matters into my own hands". A month later after the cheating situation, I received a call from another lady saying that my husband had slept with her last week when he told me that he was going to work. She texted me pictures of the two of them kissing. My heart dropped and I began to become furious. While my husband was in the bed sleeping, I went to the kitchen and got the biggest butcher knife that I could find, and I went to our bedroom, opened the door, and stood over my husband with the knife in my hands for 5 minutes, picturing how many times I was going to stab him. As soon as I lifted my

It Is Me...
The Breaking of the Generational Curse

hands to stab him in the chest, the doorbell rang back to back and they began to bang on the door. I ran to the front door angrily and asked, "Who The Hell Is It"!? It was my Elder Pat from my church. She said, "Shawna, please put the knife down and open the door"! When I opened the door I said, "How did you know that I had a knife in my hand, and what are you doing here?" She said, "The Holy Spirit sent me over here." As I began to weep harder, she began to hug me and took the knife out of my hand. Elder Pat said, "I know baby, you are hurt but this is not the answer, and God wants to free you from a spirit of anger and unforgiveness if you let him." We prayed and cried for about 1 hour, she left when my husband woke up. My husband never knew that God had just spared his life. I still was not ready to give God my anger, so when my husband went to work that day, I set his van on fire and called the fire department and reported that it was on fire, having no

It Is Me...
The Breaking of the Generational Curse

clue who could have done this. When my daughter woke up that morning, I told her to help and bring me some of her father's clothes. When she did, I put them in a pile, and I poured bleach all over his clothes. My daughter was asking questions and I told her to shut up and do what I told her to do. Doing all of this in front of my child, while making her help me pour bleach on his clothes. The sad thing about this is I still did not feel like I had an anger problem. Boosting and bragging to my friends what I did. They were all giving me high fives, which made me feel so cool and untouchable, instead of them telling me the truth. All the time still running from God and not allowing him to deliver me. After my divorce, I began dating another guy and found out that he was married, I had no idea. When I found out I kicked in his door and had about 16 other people with me. I was dressed in all black and I beat the man until he was unrecognizable. I tried to kill him, it was the grace of

It Is Me...
The Breaking of the Generational Curse

God that he did not die, and he did not press charges against me. God still kept me.

I was dating another guy who was not who he said that he was and I hit him with my car. That behavior was not acceptable, period. But I kept telling myself that this is who I am. Finally, God had to get my attention, and when God showed me myself and who I had become was UGLY in his sight. I began to repent and ask God to forgive me and to restore me into the right fellowship with Him. During that process, I had to learn to forgive myself. I asked the Lord to teach me how to respond to others without going off and being ready to fight! I have a boldness that I'm not scared of anyone, but that does not give me the right to treat people anyway I choose, and when they hurt me or offend me, I try to hurt or kill them.

I began to study the word angry and the meaning of anger. For me, the Lord showed me that I was so angry because I

It Is Me...
The Breaking of the Generational Curse

have not dealt with the past hurt of children teasing me about my skin color when I was a little. I used to be called fat, black, and ugly. I was even called that by the three men who I loved the most: My father, grandfather, and great grandfather. What I discovered was that I covered up my pain and hurt and began to take it out on others, to the point that I could have killed someone. All I can say is, "But God!" He truly had a purpose and plan for my life.

I began to read and study God's Word to help me break this generational cycle and curse of anger over my life. James 1:20 NIV "Human anger dies not to produce the righteousness of God's desires." I began to say this scripture every day and I continue to say the scripture because it helps me to stay focused on how God wants me to represent Him and give Him glory. God wants us to live and be holy. When you do not face your sin or whatever you are battling, you can never be free from it. I did not tell

It Is Me...
The Breaking of the Generational Curse

you my past to glorify it or give praise to it. I wanted to let you know that God is a deliverer, He is a Savior. God could have allowed me to go to jail for the things I did, or he could have taken my life right then. But he has a purpose and a plan for me. The Word of God says that we are overcome by our testimony. Jesus came to seek and save the lost, and I thank Him for going to the cross for my sins. Understanding what your trigger points are and writing them down will help you walk in deliverance. When the devil tries to get you off your square you will know how to stand on the word of God. It's okay to get therapy. I saw a therapist for anger management 10 different times, but once I finally made up my mind that I'm going to stand on the Word of God, understanding that Jesus went to the cross for my anger, and it no longer has me bound. That is when I became set free. The Bible says, "Whatever we bound on earth we bound in heaven!" I did not want to be bound

It Is Me...
The Breaking of the Generational Curse

anymore. I had to shift my mind and my thought process. The Bible says, "Whatever a man thinks so is he." Writing scriptures down about anger and memorizing them helped me to walk in deliverance, peace, and liberty while understanding when I must walk away from a situation so that I will not sin against God. Proverbs 15:1 NIV A gentle answer turns away wrath, but a harsh word stirs up anger. Ecclesiastes 7:9 NIV Do not be quickly provoked in your spirit, for anger resides in the lap of fools. The Word of God is a healer; Jesus came to seek and save the lost. It was through his blood that I'm free and saved. Jesus said, lay all your burdens down and He will give you rest.

Jesus could have given up one when I was in my mess, but he did not. While reading this chapter, you might be saying to yourself that your sin is too big, or God will not forgive you or He will not take away that addiction that you are battling. I'm here to tell you that God is a Deliverer, a

It Is Me...
The Breaking of the Generational Curse

Healer, Provider, Savior. He is I AM that I AM. Listen, if He did it for me, my daddy, grandfather and great grandfather, he will do it for you. Now, I'm not saying that I'm perfect, but I strive every day to be like Jesus. He is the greatest example of how to love thy neighbor as thyself. Jesus wants us to live and not die, and when you walk in anger or anything that you did not purchase you are not living, you are bound. God wants us to prosper even as our soul prospers.

If you are tired of carrying all of your burdens on your shoulders, and you have not asked Jesus Christ to come into your heart, or you may have backslid and you want to get back in right fellowship with the Lord Jesus Christ, say these words, *Lord Jesus I acknowledge that I am a sinner, and I have turned my back on you. Please come into my heart and be the head and the ruler of my life, I believe that you died on the cross for my sins and that you rose on the*

It Is Me...
The Breaking of the Generational Curse

third day. That you are sitting at the right hand of the Father. Thank you, Jesus, for saving me and coming onto my heart.

I want to welcome you into the family of God! Hallelujah, thank you Jesus, we welcome you into the family of God! I pray that you join a Bible-believing church that is going to grow spiritually. Remember, whoever the Son sets free is free indeed.

It Is Me...
The Breaking of the Generational Curse

It Is Me...
The Breaking of the Generational Curse

Chapter Five

Breaking Generational Curses Through Salvation

Dr. Stacy L. Henderson

It Is Me...
The Breaking of the Generational Curse

Dr. Stacy L. Henderson,

a native of Savannah, Georgia, is a retired Naval Officer with over 25 years of military service and experience. She is a Christian Educator, Inspirational Speaker, Businesswoman and an International Best-Selling Author. She speaks four languages and has publications in more than 40 language translations - two of which are in the White House Library. Her *Stacy's Stocking Stuffers* Christmas Charity has provided toys, meals, coats, clothing and monetary support for families around the world since 1991 and her Scholarships have financed college education for many recipients, as well. She has countless military and civilian accolades.

Stacy shares her life experiences and relies on faith-based doctrines to motivate and inspire others to achieve their best mental, physical and spiritual health. She is a Dean of Christian Leadership Schools at Christ Temple Baptist Church, Markham, Illinois and maintains close ties with her lifelong Church Family at Little Bryan Baptist Church, Savannah, Georgia. She has Degrees in Education, Health Services Management, Christian Leadership and Business Administration. A Proverbs 31 Woman, she utilizes her Spiritual Gifts to glorify God and edify His people. She is a loving Wife, proud Mother of two adult children (KeiSha and William) and several bonus children, and a doting Grandmother, comprising a blessed and beautiful 'Blended and Extended' Family. To God be the Glory!

It Is Me...
The Breaking of the Generational Curse

Contact information:
P. O. Box 886913 Great Lakes, IL 60088
or
240 Peachtree Street NW #56850 Atlanta, GA 30343

Email - Drstacylhenderson@gmail.com
Facebook - Stacy L. Henderson
Instagram - @SLHenderson007

It Is Me...
The Breaking of the Generational Curse

Breaking Generational Curses Through Salvation

A common occurrence in life is the stigma of 'generational curses.' When I hear about them or think about them, my mind does not focus on what my parents, grandparents or others before them *did* or *did not* do...I immediately think about the actions of my first parents: Adam and Eve. Romans 5:18 reads, *"So one man's sin brought guilt to all people. In the same way, one right act made people right with God. That one right act gave life to all people."* Adam's sin in the Garden of Eden initiated a curse that affects every generation. And, Romans 5:12 reminds me that *"Wherefore, as by one man sin entered into the world, and death by sin; and so death passed upon all men, for that all have sinned."* As a result, each of us remains a

It Is Me...
The Breaking of the Generational Curse

slave of sin - unless we are set free through redemption from Jesus Christ (Romans 6:20-22).

So, when it comes to the 'generational curse,' we must look deeper than just our physical family. As we are all created by the same God, we are all connected to Adam. Therefore, when Adam broke God's commandment, we were condemned with him. However, by the grace of God, we are delivered from the wage of sin - which is death - by way of salvation. Just as we were *in Adam* when he fell from grace, if we believe in Jesus, we are *in Christ* through faith. The Apostle Paul makes that point when he tells us that *"For as by one man's disobedience many were made sinners, so by the obedience of one shall many be made righteous."* (Romans 5:19).

We are all individuals with our own values and belief systems. Yet, we all have characteristics that 'run in our

It Is Me...
The Breaking of the Generational Curse

family.' For example, certain behaviors, just like certain physical attributes, are often found throughout generations: height, hair or eye color, skin tone and even the way we walk or talk. In the same way, certain types of sin can pass from generation to generation. But, curses are not irreversible. Every individual is responsible for their own choices, just as Adam was. We have free will and that influences our behaviors.

In my opinion, generational curses can be broken through faith in God. Our faith is made whole by way of salvation through Jesus Christ. I believe that when we are faced with trials in life, we have the resources needed to deal with them. We have the Word of God as a guide to help us navigate the troubled waters in life. Spiritual deliverance is available to anyone who earnestly calls upon the name of the Lord (Romans 10:13). And when we are in need of

It Is Me...
The Breaking of the Generational Curse

practical, professional help, pastors, counselors and physicians are equipped with resources to assist us.

In the end, the choice to make 'generational curses' is an individual one - so it is up to you. When reflecting on 'general curses', I take this into consideration:

- Rejecting God and spending eternity separated from Him (Matthew 8:12, Matthew 13:42) is a conscious choice. Death as a result of sin would be due to my own disobedience NOT because of the 'skeletons' in my family's closet. I must accept and understand my denial of God's forgiveness and grace, along with a refusal of His salvation through Jesus Christ (John 1:17, John 3:16) would lead to my downfall - not a 'generational curse.'

- By receiving God, I will live forever in fellowship with Him. In doing so I can avoid the mistakes that

It Is Me...
The Breaking of the Generational Curse

previous generations made, starting with Adam. Thus, I will receive God's merciful offer of unmerited deliverance and salvation.

- No one can make these decisions for you. Not your parents, grandparents, any other relatives or friends. It is solely *your* decision to make. Through Jesus Christ, the worst offender in a long line of sinners can be saved.

In summary, 'generational curses' go far beyond just what I see in my family; it started with Adam. When he fell from grace, I fell right along with him. And to this day, I continue to fall short of the Glory of God. As a human, my sinful nature makes me imperfect and unrighteous. yet, I am made perfect and receive righteousness through Christ Jesus, as a result of my unwavering faith in God and

It Is Me...
The Breaking of the Generational Curse

redemption through Jesus Christ. Generational curses can be broken through salvation. *To God Be The Glory!*

It Is Me...
The Breaking of the Generational Curse

It Is Me...
The Breaking of the Generational Curse

Chapter Six

Free From the Opinions of Others

Dr. Tamika L. Johnson

It Is Me...
The Breaking of the Generational Curse

My name is ***Dr. Tamika L. Johnson***, Ph.D. I'm a high school English Teacher, Minister, Author, Entrepreneur, and a Master Life Coach. I have a Bachelor of Education degree, a Master of Education degree, and an earned Doctor of Philosophy degree in Christian Counseling. I'm an author of more than 5 published books. All my published books can be purchased on Amazon.

I'm also a wife of 15 years and the mother of two children, ages 12 and 23. I am the founder and owner of the women's organization, Women Leaving the Clubs and Returning Home located in Milwaukee, WI. I'm also the owner of Grow Up: Empowerment Life Coaching LLC located in Germantown, WI. I'm a firm believer of living my life's purpose by bearing fruit through commitment and goal setting. My life's motto is "I will die empty." That means I will accomplish all that God has predestined for me to accomplish in the land of the living. I'm ambitious and purpose driven. I motivate others to love themselves and to walk in their purpose.

I believe in protecting my peace at all costs. I believe we all have what it takes to do what we desire to do. It's never too late for us to **DREAM BIG** and execute our goals!

My Contact Info:

Website: www.growupempowerment.com

It Is Me...
The Breaking of the Generational Curse

Email: tamika@growupempowerment.com

YouTube Channel: Grow Up On Purpose with Dr. Tamika

It Is Me...
The Breaking of the Generational Curse

Free From the Opinions of Others

There's no validation like that which comes from God and from loving yourself. Learning to love yourself is essential on this journey we call life. I also learned that loving yourself comes with a price. I spent most of my life desiring to be accepted and loved by others. I then, realized love outside of myself proves to be detrimental to my life's purpose and stifling to my growth and development. How do you break the stigma of being called "Big mouth", or being told you "Talk too much", "You're mean" or being called "Bad girl" as a child? How do you move passed the negative energy you felt from those you love and from those who are supposed to love you? Well, I moved passed those feelings by loving myself, discovering my purpose,

It Is Me...
The Breaking of the Generational Curse

learning who God called me to be, and by discerning what God has called me to do.

I learned to be okay with being me, Tamika, who she is and who God created her to be. Along this journey God spoke to me and said, "you are fearfully and wonderfully made." He created and loved my big mouth and all. As a child I often wondered why was I so opinionated and so misunderstood? I was a child who questioned everything. When adults would make comments about me and demand I listen, I was the child who asked, "Who?", "What?", "When?", "Where?", "How?", and "Why?" In my generation, a child who asked questions and who was very opinionated, was considered "disrespectful". It was never my intentions to "talk back" or to be "disrespectful". However, as a result of my "mouth" and assertive disposition, I was given names like "Big mouth

It Is Me...
The Breaking of the Generational Curse

Lucy", "Disrespectful", "Fast", and "Bad girl"; just to name a few. Although I appeared to embrace those names, I didn't quite understand the negative feelings I felt when being called those names. I learned at an early age to defend myself. Even as a child I felt the need to protect myself from those who were outside of me. I created defense mechanisms to protect myself from the negative stigmas that were being attached to who I was.

However, despite negative stigmas and names given to me by my family members, outsiders always saw something great in me. God would use my teachers, family friends, and strangers to express to me there was something special about me. God always made me feel special as well. What I didn't know was because of the negative stigmas and names given to me as a child, I would develop an insecurity of not being accepted for who I was. I didn't

It Is Me...
The Breaking of the Generational Curse

realize until I became an adult that I had begun to do for others with the hope of them loving me, seeing the best in me, and accepting me for who I was, big mouth, attitude, and all. I began to believe the love I was giving to others would be reciprocated, but it wasn't. There was a deep longing inside of me of wanting to be understood and loved. I became an overachiever with the hopes of being accepted. I began to love people who never deserved my attention with the hopes of them seeing me in a new light. I never comprehended it, but I later realized I was living off the opinions and approval of others. Not that I needed anyone to stroke my ego, I just desired not to be looked at as a bad person because of my attitude and speaking my mind. What I got in return were people taking advantage of me and my generosity. That would make me highly upset. No matter what others said about me or did to me I strived to keep my heart pure at the risk of continuing to get my

It Is Me...
The Breaking of the Generational Curse

heart broken by others. I wanted others to see me like God saw me, but they just could not. They did not have the ability to.

What my family and friends couldn't see in me, God did. God knew my heart. God knew how hard I prayed and how hard I interceded on the behalf of my family, although I felt like they were bias towards me. Because of the defense mechanisms I built to protect myself from others' opinions about me, I never really paid attention to the damage it could have caused me had I not been covered by the grace of God. No matter what others said about me, I was always reassured God loved me, so as I got older, I began to love and accept myself. As a child until adulthood, I wrote letters to God, and He answered. God was the one who continued to reassure me I was a good person and not the bad person the adults around me said I was. Even to this

It Is Me...
The Breaking of the Generational Curse

day, many say things I've learned to brush off. However, sometimes brushing things off and responding in a negative manner isn't always beneficial. I've learned everything about me is ministry related. I began to learn who I was created to be was greater than what others saw. As I grew closer to God, the effects other's opinions had on me lessened. I learned the adults around me weren't equipped to train me in the way I should go. I learned God saw the best in me when everyone else around me could only see the worst in me.

When I was a teenager and diagnosed with a lifelong illness a shift began to take place in my life. I became the "sick one". As a result of sickness and disease, other limitations were placed upon me. I used to believe people thought God allowed sickness and disease to attack my body because of me being "mean" and "disrespectful."

It Is Me...
The Breaking of the Generational Curse

However, what happened to me was nothing short of a miracle. The sickness and disease did not cause me to go astray but drew me even closer to God. It was during my teenage years my relationship with God had deepened. It was also during those years I was oftentimes hospitalized God would begin to develop in me the person I am today. As a result of God's consultation, I began to love the child I was and the person I was becoming. It all began to make sense to me. My character, my "big mouth" and my assertiveness was all a part of God's plan. It was during those times God spoke to me and said what others were calling "big mouth" was actually the projection He needed from me to fulfill my calling. The attitude others felt I had was exactly the assertiveness God needed and would use to elevate me. God desired to free me from the opinions of others by impressing on me His love for who I was right then and there. God loved me for who I was. As a result, I

It Is Me...
The Breaking of the Generational Curse

began to love and appreciate God more. I also began to love myself more and appreciate who God predestined me to be.

A true transformation took place in my life. Transformation is a change from the heart. Transformation is a real change from the inside out. I no longer had a desire to convince anyone I wasn't a bad person, it showed. I didn't have to convince anyone there was a calling on my life, it showed. The evidence of what God had been doing all along through me was showing and I didn't have to say anything. I learned I couldn't stop people from talking behind my back, lying on me, and making slanderous comments about me, but I could control my response. In no way do I allow anyone the right to disrespect me, but that is not my fight. I leave that to God. God freed me from the

It Is Me...
The Breaking of the Generational Curse

limitations that were placed upon me and from the opinions of others.

In my most recent years, those feelings of being inadequate began to creep back up. In my church and even in my workplace, those spirits of torment tried to rear their ugly heads again. Immediately, I recognized the tormenting spirits to be familiar, yet, and still their audacity would upset me. However, God continues to remind me I am free and don't have to prove anything to anyone anymore. I recently experienced a deeper level of freedom from the acceptance and opinions of others. For example, now that God has elevated me in business and ministry, I started to feel like the support I gave to others was not being reciprocated. For a while it bothered me. I felt myself becoming bitter and upset. Those feelings I felt as a child began to resurface. However, the Holy Spirit reminded me

It Is Me...
The Breaking of the Generational Curse

those thoughts and feelings were only distractions. God spoke loud and clear and said, *"YOU ARE ENOUGH!"* I had to learn to love myself at another level. I had to learn to love myself even if it meant I'll stand alone. I had to, once again, learn no matter what level God was taking me to, He is my source of contentment. It's His approval that matters. I, once again, embraced the love God has always expressed to me. As a result, I began to love myself at a deeper level. I am freer than I have ever been. I am free from the opinions of church folks, family members, and so-called friends. God loves me. I love me and that is all that matters!

Do I desire to be loved by others? Yes, everyone does, but not to the point of it hindering me and stifling my journey. Everyone desires to love and to be loved. However, true love doesn't usually come until you learn to love yourself unconditionally. I realized I always had a

It Is Me...
The Breaking of the Generational Curse

sense of love for myself, even as a child, that's why I wouldn't allow people to treat me any kind of way. However, as an adult I understand in loving myself, it may not cause others to love me, but they will respect me. On this journey of being free from the opinions of others, I've learned to grow some thick skin. I learned this world is full of hurt people and 'hurt people' hurt people. Some people may never understand the impact their words have on a person's life until it's too late. What I've learned is not everyone I love is equipped to love me the way I need to be loved. Only God can love me the way I need to be loved.

I am *FREE!* Whom the Son sets free is truly FREE INDEED! Not to sound cocky or anything, but because of my assertiveness and my ability to advocate for myself as a child, I now spend my life advocating for others. Although I desired the love I gave, it really doesn't even matter

It Is Me...
The Breaking of the Generational Curse

anymore. I've learned there is Greater work for me to do. The girl my family demonized by calling her "big mouth Lucy", "disrespectful", "bad girl" and saying "you talk too much" is still growing in the Lord and walking confidently in her purpose. The girl whose name they slandered is now a Doctor of Philosophy. My big mouth and attitude were a part of God's plan for my life since my creation. God spoke to me one day and told me to say to whomever calls me "big mouth" that He created me with this *BIG MOUTH* and to let them know I have something important to say if they would just listen...lol... "Big Mouth Lucy" is now Dr. Tamika. "Big Mouth Lucy" has been a teacher for over 20 years. Tamika is also a minister. I also advocate on the behalf of those whose voices have been silenced. Who would I be if I allowed the naysayers to silence me as a child? I know I wouldn't be the person I am today. God saw the best in me when everyone else around me could

It Is Me...
The Breaking of the Generational Curse

only see the worst in me. Not only did I begin my teaching career at the age of 23 years old, at the age of 43 I earned my Doctor of Philosophy Degree as well. "Bad Girl" is now a Teacher, Minister, Life Coach, Motivational Speaker, Author, and Doctor of Philosophy. God has called me for such a time as this and *I LOVE IT!* My confidence comes from the Lord and is in Him and no one else! This year, the year of 2021, I've reached a new level of freedom from the opinions of others, and I am just fine with it!!

What I also learned on my journey to freedom from the opinions of others was elevation sometimes requires separation. Since I've been at this new level of loving myself and being okay with where God has taken me in life, I had to remove some people from my sphere. I've learned when people don't love themselves or are stuck in life, they'll try to rub that same energy off on you and if

It Is Me...
The Breaking of the Generational Curse

you aren't sure about who you are, you'll embrace it. I'm okay with being Tamika. I love my "big mouth", attitude and all! I'm okay with loving myself even if I'm loving myself alone. I refuse to remain where I am tolerated and not celebrated. If people want to speak negatively about me or slander me, they are welcome to do it away from me. Because I love myself and I am free, I dare not allow anyone who's toxic near me. I have a right to protect my peace at all costs. If others can't or refuse to see me the way God sees me, it's their lost. I have decided I will love like Christ love, and I will remain free from the opinions of others at all costs! As a Life Coach, Minister, Teacher, Motivational Speaker, and Author, I've learned if my family and so-called friends don't support me, God will send strangers to. I will impact those I'm supposed to impact. I am here to do the will of God, not to please everyone. I understand my calling is for me and the

It Is Me...
The Breaking of the Generational Curse

services I provide aren't for everyone. Jesus said that

Greater works will I do, and *I AM HERE FOR IT!*

In conclusion, I will share a poem written on my behalf by my husband, Dontre "Loud Thoughtz" Johnson. This poem depicts my life's story.

UNVEILED

Stop trying to make me something that I'm not,

the picture that you paint is far from a Picasso - I see your plot.

There is no beauty in it

though you're entitled to your opinion you've overextended it,

you've stepped into the realm of embellishment.

Am I Saint or Salvage (Savage),

or have the two intertwined and combined - making me a Maverick?

I'm a sinner because I was born into a world of sin,

not because of any act perpetrated with my hands.

Or because of anything that's been conceived in my heart

sure, I contemplated the thought but then I ripped it apart.

It Is Me...
The Breaking of the Generational Curse

I'm not a person with two heads whose actions are dichotomized,

a monster who speaks with a fork tongue consumed with lies.

I'm just plain old me; stop pointing at me,

I'm a child of the Most High God, His anointing is on me!!

It Is Me...
The Breaking of the Generational Curse

It Is Me...
The Breaking of the Generational Curse

Chapter Seven

The Restoration of All Things

Mind, Spirit, Body, and Soul

Shalonda Danette Taylor- Earl

It Is Me...
The Breaking of the Generational Curse

Shalonda Danette Taylor was born November 3, 1970, in Gary, Indiana. I'm the oldest of seven children in my family. I'm the mother of four children and eleven grandchildren, and I was also a foster parent for twenty-three children in three years. I have supported many families in crises. I moved to Milwaukee, Wisconsin March 1993, and I became a believer in that same year. I am a Pastor, Prophetess, Spiritual Advisor, and I have worked in early childhood development for twenty-seven years. I received an associate's and bachelor's degree in theology. I specialized in working with youth that had Autism.

Some of the businesses that I own are The Mahogany Collection by Shalonda and Timeless Kouture Soapbox. I have outreach ministries, Sego Outreach Ministries, and Voice of The Intercessor. I'm Vice President of Kingdom Genesis Ministries since 2009. I have traveled throughout the USA and Guatemala as a prophetic end-time voice. I have been preaching and teaching a fiery message and birthing healing, and freedom throughout the nations.

I was the only person to have a Youth Revival on Capitol Court Grounds. The event was a Youth Explosion 2000 and, I have taught teen bible study. Teaching the youth of all ages how to hear the voice of God and I have done many prophetic activations. I have facilitated at least twenty community prayer walks throughout the

It Is Me...
The Breaking of the Generational Curse

community. I have a healing and deliverance ministry specializing in personal body ministry. God called me to be an intercessor and, I have been an intercessor for over twenty-eight years. I use Prayer strategies, meditation, prophetic declarations and, I've seen results globally.

I'm serving as a global humanitarian that builds leaders and strengthening family structures in this world. I am a marriage and relationship counselor. I was married for twenty years, and I continue to have a fruitful marriage and relationship ministry. I am the founder of The Voice of the Intercessor and, I currently can be seen on Roku TV. The Voice of the Intercessor is on Roku TV "World Events and Bible Prophecy Channel. I'm a facilitator on the Kingdom Genesis prayer line every Tuesday at 9 p.m.

It Is Me...
The Breaking of the Generational Curse

The Restoration of All Things

Mind, Spirit, Body, and Soul

As a builder of the Kingdom of God, I understand the responsibility of healing for my generation. The hearts of women in my family were yoked up and paralyzed by fear for many years, even decades. We were bound and without hope, until I began to unravel through scriptures, meditation, and prayer releasing, the promises of God. We began to experience healing in every area of our lives. God's will is for us to be whole in mind, spirit, body, and soul. Restoration means to restore. The biblical meaning of the word restoration is to receive back in abundance what was lost and receive everything greater than its original state. The restoration of all things, mind, spirit, body, and soul, speaks directly to the beginning of creation

It Is Me...
The Breaking of the Generational Curse

in Genesis. In Genesis, God the creator crafted all things in his image and likeness. We were created without flaw or defect as we journey through life obstacles sometimes, there is deep-rooted trauma. When we become conscious of the trauma in our life, we are responsible for sorting through the emotional damage to a place of wholeness where nothing is misaligned or broken.

I am a mother of three daughters and eight granddaughters. My greatest desire for my girls is complete restoration, healing, and freedom of all generational bondages. I deliberately began to pray, purchase books, and research on how to break generational curses in the bloodline. As I started praying about my struggles, I discovered fear was at the root of every matter in my life, and it needed to be uprooted by the roots. Restoration is a process and, I am returning to my original state before I was damaged. As a fifty-year-old woman, I have experienced many of the same

It Is Me...
The Breaking of the Generational Curse

hurdles as my foremother's, such as sexual abuse, child abuse, teenage pregnancy, broken relationships, rape, mental health issues, and excessive spending rooted in the spirit of fear. The bible says that fear brings torment and, there were people in the bible that had experienced great distresses. It was a direct correlation of their mental, spiritual, and emotional bondage reflected in their actions. For example, the paralytic man at the pool of Bethesda suffered for thirty-eight years. He was waiting for his opportunity to be healed but, having no one to help him. He needed divine intervention, so Jesus steps in and invites him to the cleansing waters that healed his mind, spirit, body, and soul in John 5:1-15 (paraphrased version).
In my studies, I discovered that my mental clarity was essential and that I am the governor of my thoughts. It is my thought's that produces my actions. My actions are what frame my world. Our upbringing directly or

It Is Me...
The Breaking of the Generational Curse

indirectly affects our decisions, attitudes, and behaviors. The many years of abuse caused me to be distant, angry, and afraid to communicate with others for fear of rejection. I began to use scripture references and, I turned them into prayers. Now my prayer life started to flourish. Prayer became an intimate outlet that I could use anytime, anyplace, and anywhere. The book of psalms spoke to my soul, strengthening my spirit and providing me with great direction for my life. As I prayed, I desperately searched for inner peace, a place to belong, and my purpose in life. Knowing that I am fearfully and wonderfully complexed yet made in the image and likeness of God. In the restoration of all things, I needed to put my person (my body, mind, spirit, and soul) in a state of wholeness. I needed to change my mind concerning negative thoughts, feelings, and emotions. The scripture references that the way a man thinketh in his heart so is he.

It Is Me...
The Breaking of the Generational Curse

My relational life changed very quickly because I reevaluated how I interacted with others in uncomfortable situations then, I decided to change my environment for the better. What I am thinking about matters when I thought about great things then, great things started happening. This mindset became my pattern of thinking and, it has caused a paradigm shift. My commitment to change manifested through positive affirmations, praying, and meditating on scriptures. I am a mountain mover as I hurdled through the heaviest weights in life. It was essential for me to identify how to move the mountain of fear out of my mental and emotional condition. When the spirit of fear is in your life, it holds up blessings, slows down progress, and eventually paralyzes the mind, the spirit, the body, and the soul. That is why the bible gently reminds us that if you are battling and struggling with the spirit of fear, it does not come from God! But he has given

It Is Me...
The Breaking of the Generational Curse

us power, love, and a sound mind to return to wholeness. I had a Psalm 23:3 experience. God began to restore my soul as I forgave my enemies, released past hurts and pains, weeping with deep joy as the light behind the mountain had started to shine on every area of my life. At this time now my heart had filled with strength and unconditional love.

I am freedom the power of forgiveness grants me freedom. I have accepted responsibility for my decisions personally, socially, emotionally, interpersonally, psychologically, or environmentally. It is my freedom that breaks generational bondages and releases generational blessings within my bloodline. It is the freedom that is imperative in the restoration of all things as God restores my soul. He is bringing me back to the path of right living for his namesake.

He brought back my soul and led me on the path of freedom and truth. I was married for twenty years it ended

It Is Me...
The Breaking of the Generational Curse

with a nasty divorce. I had one miscarriage in my life. I was homeless two times. I got arrested during a kid's birthday party and, a foreclosure, bankruptcies, and repossessions are what I have experienced in my life. I received my high school diploma at forty-six years old. My father is still missing since 1999, diagnosed with cancer in 2017, experienced a flash fire, two rapes, and mental and emotional breakdowns to maintain my soundness of mind, prayer, meditation, and speaking out loud daily.

These are the following declarations that are necessary to receive freedom. I receive in my mind, body, spirit, and soul restoration of all things. I decree and declare the spirit of fear is broken right now from my bloodline and, every generation of women in my family will walk in peace, love, and joy. As we maintain a kingdom-driven attitude, I claim mental and emotional freedom in Jesus's Name that gives

It Is Me...
The Breaking of the Generational Curse

us the mind, thoughts, and desires to walk in a Christ-like way. Amen

It Is Me...
The Breaking of the Generational Curse

It Is Me...
The Breaking of the Generational Curse

Chapter Eight

My Healing Was Connected to My Forgiveness

Pastor Morgana Matthews

It Is Me...
The Breaking of the Generational Curse

Pastor Morgana Matthews, Born and raised on the south-side of Chicago a mother of four beautiful daughters. I Was introduced to the Lord at a young age but it didn't become real to me until my early twenties. Following my mother, I Moved to Milwaukee where I began to hear from the Lord regarding the mantle He has on my life.

He began to unfold His Word to me and showed me in John 12:32 that if He be lifted up from the earth, He would draw all men unto HIM. Under the leadership of Apostle Lock Sr. I began to evangelize and spread the Word, lifting up the name of Jesus and drawing souls to glorify the kingdom of God.

Under the leadership of the bishop Burt, I was the lead over the outreach ministry, I taught and preached there for five years. Under the leadership of bishop Oilphant I was Pastor of outreach, Sunday school teacher, and served on the hospitality team. As a visionary and Bible teacher, preacher, author, and Conference speaker. I continue to serve God in my own ministry which is Sent by God outreach ministries.

I Continue to serve the people as God serves me. I believe Numbers 23:19 that says God is not a man, that He should lie; neither the son of man, that He should repent: Hath He said, and shall He not do it? Or hath he spoken, and shall

It Is Me...
The Breaking of the Generational Curse

He not make it good? As I travel, I continue to seek God for what He is doing in this season for His people and preaching and teaching Gods Holy Word wherever I go.

It Is Me...
The Breaking of the Generational Curse

My Healing Was Connected to My Forgiveness

There is no manual given to parents when they start having kids. Parents give us who they are and their experiences. There are no perfect parents. If you want to raise children who have an identity problem, self-esteem issues and are broken from the inside out, then be the type of parents who don't take your parenting seriously.

Think about it... We get our thought process, values, principles, and identity from our parents. They teach us early in life to be a certain way. The flip side is those parents who are emotionally, Spiritually, and mental balanced raise those kinds of children. You get what you are not what you desire... My point is, how and who you are raised by has a great impact on how you turn out.

It Is Me...
The Breaking of the Generational Curse

Parenting is not for everyone. When God blesses you to have children, that is a gift. Some women can't have children. On these next few pages, I'm going to discuss with you the childhood of three children who were affected differently but in life-altering ways by a mother who was truly broken and should not have had any children in the state she was in. And unfortunately, a father who was never there. I can hear your thoughts, *Then I could have never been born, you are right and I'm grateful I was born for such a time as this*. IT IS ME! I am the generational curse breaker. The buck stops with me!! I said I didn't want this for my adult life. I wanted to be a good parent to my children. What is a generational curse? I'm glad you asked. It is a passing down of sinful behavior that gets replicated in the next generation. Parents don't just pass down physical attributes, but also Spiritual and emotional attributes as well. I could go deeper but we will leave it

It Is Me...
The Breaking of the Generational Curse

here for now. I want you to get a simple explanation of generational curses. It's sins that are in our bloodline. Things that happened in our family tha*t were not* dealt with regarding our brokenness. There is no shame in asking for help. My aunts and uncles were very private regarding our family's dysfunction. How sad because they did not want to talk about it, their lives were impacted by it. I can only speak for my culture on this, black people for the most part, don't believe in mental illness and sharing their issues with others. The devil is a liar. If something bad happens in this house that damages me, I've got to get help. It is insanity to keep doing the same thing expecting a different response. If we want something different, we have to do something different. When we continue to go along to get along, nothing changes. The curse is then passed down to future generations. Deuteronomy 28:15-68 gives us fifty-three generational curses. When you have an opportunity, look at

It Is Me...
The Breaking of the Generational Curse

the list of curses listed there. I have to admit, generational curses are real. Let me prove it to you Hebrews 9:22 New King James version says, "And according to the law almost all things are purified with blood, and without shedding of blood there is no remission." A generational curse comes through our family bloodline, and it can only be broken through the bloodline of Jesus. Thank God for the blood of Jesus, the blood still works. When we say, "Satan, the Blood of Jesus is against you," we render the enemy useless!! I want you to repeat after me, *Satan, the Blood of Jesus is against you. You can't have my family, faith, focus, or purpose in the name of JESUS.* In doing so, you, by faith, reverse the curse. The curse is no longer when you plead the Blood of Jesus. When I was growing up as a child, the level The dysfunction in which I was raised was insane; no one seemed to care about changing it either.

It Is Me...
The Breaking of the Generational Curse

You must be very careful with not getting too comfortable with dysfunction. I learned early that my mother had a lot of personal demons she was dealing with. She was a very heavy drug user. She went from smoking crack to shooting up. I remember I was fourteen and walking in the bathroom seeing my mom on the toilet with a needle hanging from her arm. I really had a slight hatred towards her. I Watched my mother destroy her own life and almost destroyed all of her children. I've come to understand in a real way, what you don't deal with will utterly destroy you from the inside out. You are alive on the outside but dead on the inside. When your heart is in pieces and you feel like you are not worthy, you begin to self-Sabotage. We were all affected by my mom's behavior. My brother went to jail and battled with homosexuality doing things to try and survive. My sister has a spirit of indifference. She made her boyfriend shoot her neighbor in front of the ladies' kids because she

It Is Me...
The Breaking of the Generational Curse

called her the 'B' word true story. This happened in Milwaukee. It is a fact that hurt people, hurt people. My issue was that I came close to becoming the thing I hated. I didn't have a drug issue, but I was numb. I felt nothing. My way of coping was survival mode; I'm going to get you before you get me. I would flip men like I changed underwear and I did that every day. I wasn't a whore that walked up and down the street but that was my mentality. No money, no honey!! I was born and raised on the south side of Chicago so I was a force to be reckoned with. I went to Hyde Park Career Academy from 1984-1988. School was my outlet; I met some really cool kids there and that allowed me to be exposed to something positive. If God chooses not to take you out of a situation, He stays with you while you go through it. My mother had really started to just get out of control leaving us alone for days. Then when she came back home, she was high and

It Is Me...
The Breaking of the Generational Curse

would pull me out of bed and start beating me for no reason. She never did that to my siblings. I've always felt like Joseph in my family. I was always different; to a large degree I didn't let what happened to me get in me and I know that was the Grace of God. The devil had a plot but God had a plan. Thank God for a praying grandmother who would take me to church with her on Sundays. God's hand has always been in my life. I didn't know it then, but I am totally aware of it now. God protected me in a toxic environment. I never questioned God about why He gave me one parent who was broken and the other absent. I believe that God gives HIS toughest battles to those He chooses to use as deliverers and healers. When God takes hold of our hearts, He is the game changer. My mom was sick and I moved here to take care of her; you heard me right, the woman who only gave birth to me.

It Is Me...
The Breaking of the Generational Curse

I relocated to Milwaukee with my kids. The Bible is clear on how we are supposed to treat our parents and I honored that. The Holy Spirit enabled me to show my mom grace. It wasn't easy. I had to keep praying for her and my siblings. Prayer helps you to forgive those who hurt you. Exodus 14:14 says, "The Lord will fight for me, if I hold my peace. I believe in the Word of God." Give people to God and live a free life. We try to do too much in our own strength. When we really do what the scriptures tell us we are better off. The enemy loves for us to get entangled in unforgiveness. I battled with it for years. I believe that's why I have joint issues. Unforgiveness is like me drinking the poison, expecting the offender to die. I married a man with that same spirit. When we got into a confrontation, we were like two pit bulls in a cage with one piece of meat. Unforgiveness kills everything it encounters: relationships, marriages, and church unity. Luke 17 tells us it is

It Is Me...
The Breaking of the Generational Curse

impossible for us not to be offended. We have to learn how to let go and let God. The Bible is clear that if we don't forgive God won't forgive us. Matthew 18:21-25 is a must read for those who battle with this spirit. When you have experienced a lot of trauma and rejection you tend to shut down and go inward. I want to help you today. The enemy is having a field day with the saints because they are so easily offended, which leads to unforgiveness if it is not handled properly. The believer who harbors bitterness in his or her heart is giving Satan a foothold in your life. Unresolved anger, if not checked, will also lead to unforgiveness. The Bible tells us in Ephesians 4:26-27, "Be angry and do not sin; do not let the sun go down on your anger and give no opportunity to the devil.

Whenever God tells us not to do something it is for our own good. The devil wants you to think that God is keeping something from you. Not true. God knows the damage that

It Is Me...
The Breaking of the Generational Curse

comes with anger, bitterness, rejection, and unforgiveness. The book of Psalms is a book of emotions. God gave us emotions but we must steward them in a way that is not damaging to our core. I will also add here the antidote for dealing with anger is to let it go right away. When we keep reliving the offense and going over it in our minds that causes us to become bitter and not long after unforgiveness moves in. Luke 6:45 says, "A good man out of the good treasure of his heart bringeth forth that which is good; and an evil man out of the evil treasure of his heart bringeth forth that which is evil: for of the abundance of the heart the mouth speaketh." This scripture is so on point. Have you ever met someone, I don't care what time of the day you talk to them, who is negative and pessimistic. It is a heart issue. So, let's deal with it now if you are always cursing, gossiping, lying, bitter, and negative; you have a heart issue. The Bible says, "Out of the abundance of the

It Is Me...
The Breaking of the Generational Curse

heart the mouth speaks." Simply put if you have a problem with what comes out of your mouth, then check your heart. People try to mask it as somebody else's fault. That is why I'm responding this way which is wrong. No one can make you do anything. What typically happens is that negative emotions are already there, and it takes the right set of circumstances to expose it or cause it to come out. The human body is designed in such an amazing way that we suppress those emotions that cause us trauma or heartache. This might be a short-term remedy but long term it has disastrous effects; if not given to the Holy Spirit to help you process it correctly, it will eat you up from the inside out. You will be such a toxic person no one will want to be around you. You are bound and I'm anointed to set the captives free in Jesus' name. I'm spending a great deal of time on this so I can set free whoever reads this book. There is no distance in the spirit. When we allow these

It Is Me...
The Breaking of the Generational Curse

emotions to control us, it destroys us and our witness. Someone is always watching our lives and we have to live in such a way that if we never open our mouths our lives speak for us. When people look at your life, do they see a life yielded to Jesus?

Do they see a person who is whole and complete in themselves? Or do they see a person who is always striving to outdo the next person? Broken people have a competing spirit. They try to get degrees and material things to make them feel important or that they have arrived. I will save you some time because you have to do your work regarding your heart or mental health. I have a saying, *I'm not concerned about what you say but I'm always watching what you do.* Our do confirms what we say we believe. Finally, I want to share with you why it is imperative that we deal with our wounded hearts. The enemy loves when we are emotionally spent and tapped out. The Holy Spirit

It Is Me...
The Breaking of the Generational Curse

revealed to me a few years back to deal with my wounded heart. I was so messed up from childhood issues and adult issues that I was closed off. I felt nothing. I had a spirit of indifference but when I allowed God to show me my heart and I began to look at all I had gone through, I said to myself, *I should have been crazy but GOD*. I went to therapy for a while but ultimately it was my relationship with God that helped me to be truly healed in my emotions. LASTLY, the heart is where God accesses us and if God the creator of you and everything that exists can't get to you, then you really are in trouble. God designed us with free will. HE is not going to force us to do anything. We have to surrender and relinquish whatever it is that has us bound. Sweet Holy Spirit, I pray for all those who will read this book that they would accept Jesus as their Lord and SAVIOR and allow Him to turn their hearts of stone into hearts of flesh. He is the only one who can do it. I'm

It Is Me...
The Breaking of the Generational Curse

believing God for supernatural heart healing in Jesus' name

AMEN.

It Is Me...
The Breaking of the Generational Curse

It Is Me...
The Breaking of the Generational Curse

Chapter Nine

Disrupted By Division

Tamika Marable

It Is Me...
The Breaking of the Generational Curse

Tamika Marable is a Special Education Teacher for the Milwaukee Public School system, and reigning Mrs. Wisconsin United States 2021. She has a BA in human service with a concentration in criminal justice and a MA in Urban Special Education. She has been married to her husband Robert for 8 blessed years and they have 6 children together as a blended family.

With a heart's mission to strengthen the family unit, Tamika dedicates her time and support to engaging, encouraging, and enhancing the lives of women and girls. She understands that when women are encouraged to be their best self, strong, and healthy it creates an atmosphere for their families to better thrive. With experience in career fields such as healthcare, corrections, social work, and now education Tamika has an ultimate desire to positively impact and give back to the community that helped to shape and mold her into the woman she is today.

In July 2000, She was challenged with the devastating news that her two younger sisters accidentally drowned in a Milwaukee River. Over a period of 15 years, she has sat with this sadness and nudging in her spirit to share her story so others could be saved. In February 2020, she launched a non-profit Sisters Too Inc., in honor of her sisters with a mission to inspire women and girls to grow in their purpose as well as to educate and raise awareness on water safety and drowning prevention. To her, Sisters Too is not just a platform, but her life's mission. Water Safety

It Is Me...
The Breaking of the Generational Curse

and Drowning Prevention has become a major focus for her in hopes that not one more family would have to be devastatingly impacted by this preventable cause and/or experience a loss such as her family and so many other families have to this day.

It Is Me...
The Breaking of the Generational Curse

Disrupted By Division

When I was asked what generational curse I was breaking, I had to stop and think to myself, *Good question.* I had never really given it much thought. I then began to wonder, *What is a generational curse, anyway?* After I did a bit of googling, I concluded that it really is just choices that were made by our ancestors because of experiences, values and ideas that have been passed down to them and then unfortunately to us. I questioned myself, *Could that possibly be it?* I decided to reflect deeper within and what I am assured of is that I have a choice in all situations as an adult. I understand that no one can make a choice for me when it comes to being free from the bondage of past mistakes of my mother, father, sister, brother, myself, or any other family member connected to my family tree. I then had to ask myself these questions:

It Is Me...
The Breaking of the Generational Curse

- Was I impacted by divorce, separation, or an affair?
- Have I ever been affected by the abuse of drugs and/or alcohol in my family?
- Have I ever lived with a significant other without being married?
- Have I ever experienced death of someone close to me, including miscarriage or suicide?
- Have I ever had an abortion?
- Were my parents absent and unavailable at some points?
- Was I ever in foster care?
- What is my greatest fear?

I was dismayed by the fact that I could answer the first seven questions with a definitive yes and question eight could be answered in a way that signified that all previous questions were my greatest fears, in a way. So, I then began to wonder again what generational curse am I breaking? Has it been broken? Or is it in the process of breaking? Well, to be honest I believe that from the reflective questions above and the life experiences that I have had

It Is Me...
The Breaking of the Generational Curse

without a shadow of a doubt, division is breaking in my life. Notice I said, "breaking" because as I continue to share with you in this chapter, you will notice that division seems to still be having its way, but God will have the final say! Let's break down the meaning of division. It can be defined in several ways: first, a method of distributing a group of things into equal parts and second, the condition or an instance of being divided in opinion or interest, disagreement and disunity. For the sake of any confusion, I will be referring to the second one throughout this chapter.

I have heard stories of how and why my mother and father got divorced and it never really dawned on me that their divorce impacted my life more than I imagined. The mere fact of their separation caused me to believe that my father was a man that I had never seen before. I was always just left with a name to ponder on whenever I thought about

It Is Me...
The Breaking of the Generational Curse

where my daddy was when I was a child. You see, I would ask my mother who my father was and she gave me a name and even an image. That image stuck with me for a very long time, well into my adulthood until I found out he was not my father. My father was her husband, the one that she separated herself from. Considering the circumstances, I don't blame her, but her decision had a trickle-down effect. It left our family uncovered from the protection and leadership of the male figure and role in the household. God's purpose for marriage is and has always been for two to become one, covering one another in love. I believe a father is supposed to be in a child's life to provide guidance, love, protection, discipline, support, attention, and encouragement. He is supposed to show you who you are because you came from him. Well, the absence of my father showed me the opposite. I didn't know where I came from, why my eyes were brown, why my lips were so pink,

It Is Me...
The Breaking of the Generational Curse

why I was such an optimistic little girl, and why I am who I am.

I never quite understood how I was supposed to be treated by boys, let alone men. I had to figure all of this out through lived experiences and the support of other people in my life. That level of division between my mother and father did something to me. It made me believe in something or should I say someone that wasn't really connected to me. I believe that is where the curse starts, when you start believing a lie, right? Believing a lie will cause you to make decisions you may not have made if the truth was revealed sooner. I believe this is how division is able to continue to remain in families and the lives of God's people. I believe to break this we have to be better at communicating the truth to one another in love. We have to learn to be more patient with each other as well. The truth

It Is Me...
The Breaking of the Generational Curse

of the matter is that we are all different with our own personalities, perceptions and opinions. This is actually the beauty of God's plan. When we can find a way to fit it all together like a puzzle we will be headed in the right direction, don't you think?

When my mother left my father, she brought our family here to live in Milwaukee, WI. She was a young divorced woman still learning herself and trying to figure life out. At the age of about sixteen my mother had been disfellowshipped. My grandmother was a devout Jehovah's witness and still is to this day and because of this, she disowned my mother in a way. That division between my mother and grandmother caused a trickle-down effect as well. Can you see the disruption of division roaring about? By the time my mother was thirty-eight years old she had five daughters. When I think about that, considering that I

It Is Me...
The Breaking of the Generational Curse

am thirty-eight right now with only two biological children, I can imagine the level of stress that she may have been going through and the strength required to maintain. As I became an adult, I was able to allot more understanding to the woman that I have experienced and seen through my mother. Growing up it was difficult because my mother was not always present for me as a little girl, young woman, and even today as a grown woman. As a young girl I spent time in the foster care system because my mother had personal struggles of her own. As a teenager I experienced teen pregnancy because I was often left without parental guidance, and as a young woman I experienced divorce because I chose to marry a man in hopes to heal from a dysfunctional relationship I was previously in. There goes the disruption of division rearing its ugly head yet again. When I divorced I started having self-defeating thoughts telling myself, *My son is going to*

It Is Me...
The Breaking of the Generational Curse

grow up without a father, I will never be in a healthy relationship with the opposite sex, and I will experience one of my biggest fears: being married and divorced several times over.

As I was experiencing these thoughts it brought me to a place of lack. I felt like it was nothing I could do in relationships that would be right. I remember telling the Lord that I would never get married again. I also would believe that I was a bad mother because I didn't just stay in my marriage for the sake of my son. I could go on and on, but I think you get my point. The division cycle happening in my life was beginning to take a toll on me. It was changing the way I thought about life, people, and most importantly myself. I had to really get a grip on things, and I mean that in every sense of the word. I had to start telling myself, *Tamika, you are not your past self. You will not get*

It Is Me...
The Breaking of the Generational Curse

divorced again. You are a good mother, regardless of what decision you had to make for you. Will my decisions have a trickle-down effect? Yes, everyone's actions do. You have to be willing to come to grips with the fact that you are not always going to get it right all the time, but you can strive to make the best decision for your entire family each time. I believe once we have the perspective and a mindset that most things are not just about "me", that is when we can be totally free. Free from the bondage of division and curses, free from jealousy and strife, and free from the idea that we don't have a choice to make things right.

I am going to attempt to take you all on a journey with me. I wish you could close your eyes right now, but you are reading this chapter. So that you can picture this, just think about division as a gunshot wound. For starters we know that a bullet can cause severe damage to your organs and

It Is Me...
The Breaking of the Generational Curse

tissues even if it does not hit them. We also know that a bullet can cause life threatening injuries leading up to death if it hits a main artery. In that regard, I hope you can see how detrimental the spirit of division can be. When you consider a gunshot wound there are one of three things that could happen in my perspective. One, the bullet can stay embedded in the body. Two, the bullet can be removed from the place of impact or three the bullet can come clean out on the other side. Let's explore these three options further, if you will, as it relates to division. The idea of the bullet staying embedded in the body could have lasting effects, right? Embedded means fixed firmly and deeply in a surrounding mass; implanted. The longer that the bullet stays embedded the more comfortable that the person will get in knowing that it is there. There would be no sense of urgency to remove it or maybe sometimes the person may even forget that it is there for a period of time. According

It Is Me...
The Breaking of the Generational Curse

to some doctors, it may be safer to leave a bullet in the body because removing it will cause more harm than good. This is what it looks like with division having been embedded in a family's DNA. Even when they know that it's there or that it exists, they have gotten so used to it being a part of the body that they do nothing to remove it. They may even feel like addressing it will cause more harm than good. I believe in some areas of my relationships this is what is happening. We know it's there, but it's comfortable to not address or confront it. My prayer is that it can no longer remain comfortable in my life or yours if you're reading this and can relate.

Division needs to be uprooted and a new thing planted. If this means your attitude has to change to deal with so and so, then work on you. If it means that so and so has to vent about childhood trauma and it seems dramatic, so be it.

It Is Me...
The Breaking of the Generational Curse

This is what it would look like for the bullet to be removed with the understanding that it takes the effort of all parties to reach a specific goal or connection within the body. I believe all things need to be uprooted in due season and when it's not done in a healthy way the effects can be of an even greater magnitude and purpose. Although when being "removed" it may hurt and the healing process will take time, I'm certain that this is one way to break the disruption of division in our life and families. Then if you think about the bullet coming clean out the other side this is similar to being removed but with a slight difference. The difference being you are able to see the point on entrance and exit. You will always notice that point of impact, there may even be a scar seen among everyone. The good thing about this is that you can testify about where you came from versus where you are now. Unfortunately, some people have to see the mess in order to receive the message.

It Is Me...
The Breaking of the Generational Curse

I often think about losing my younger sisters and how this created a space for the disruption of division to be continued in my family. Still to this day my relationship with my sisters, who are still in the land of the living, is basically non-existent. Not because I don't want it, but because the spirit of division has found a way to manifest itself again. I often ask myself where do I begin to try to mend this? Does it start with a phone call, an apology, or both? What if you have already tried these things? What if you don't know where the problem lies? Again, my question becomes where do I begin to mend. I have found that the answer is within, that's where you start. You start to mend from within. I realized that as I'm on the journey to breaking this generational "choice" in my life and the lives of my children, it all begins with me. This is my confession: My children will see me happy, fruitful and

It Is Me...
The Breaking of the Generational Curse

free. My children will grow up and call me blessed and they will be blessed. I am forever grateful to God that he has given me the mind of Christ. I am no longer subject to the enemy's plans and/or schemes. I am fearfully and wonderfully made, I speak healing and life over myself, family, you, and your family. I am engulfed in the truth and am aware that I only have control over myself. I cannot control the thoughts and opinions of others and I will not attempt to. I am forever grateful for the experiences that I've had in my life because they have shaped and molded me into who I am today. Upon adopting the confession and mindset above I realize division does break; it is me, breaking the generational curse. These are examples of how I am breaking the disruption of division in my life.

- Continuing to act in love and walk in truth
- Being a faithful wife and the best mother and example, I can be for my children

It Is Me...
The Breaking of the Generational Curse

- Remaining faithful in my faith
- Believing that what I speak is already done
- Forgiving others and restoring relationships

In conclusion, I believe God has a predestined purpose and plan for your life and I encourage you not to let division disrupt that. A passage of scripture that was put on my heart to share with you is Romans 5:19 - 21 from the amplified, it reads, "For just as through one man's disobedience (his failure to hear, his carelessness) the many were made sinners, so through obedience of the one man the many will be made acceptable to God and brought into right standing with him." But the Law came to increase and expand (the awareness of) the trespass (by defining and unmasking sin). But where sin increased, (God's remarkable, gracious gift of) grace (His unmerited favor) has surpassed it and increased all the more, so that, as sin reigned in death, so also grace would reign through

It Is Me...
The Breaking of the Generational Curse

righteousness which brings eternal life through Jesus Christ our Lord. Through this chapter, my hope is that you understand the concept of the right to choose righteousness. Life is full of choices, it's up to you which path you decide to take. Whatever you choose to do, I would encourage you to follow the plans of God for your life. At times you may get weary and may not know your way. It is during this time that we must lean in more to hear the Father's voice of direction and correction. In closing, I am aware that I have a choice and I will continuously choose not to repeat the cycle.

It Is Me...
The Breaking of the Generational Curse

It Is Me...
The Breaking of the Generational Curse

Chapter Ten

The Breaking of My Family's Generational Curse

Latonya Willett

It Is Me...
The Breaking of the Generational Curse

Latonya Brown Willett, a wife of 25 years, mother of 4, financial analyst, entrepreneur, motivational speaker, and Evangelist. Latonya was born on the Westside of Chicago. She's the next to youngest of 4 children. At a very early age, (4 years old) Latonya always had a caring heart for others. She would help others as much as she could by giving of her time, money, toys, and anything else she had to give.

As Latonya became older, she still had a caring spirit, but ran into life along the way. By the age of 15, she had her first child and by the time she was 17 she had her second child. While struggling to keep up her grades and take care of 2 children with the support of only her older sister, her second child would eventually die at the age of 4 months old on Mother's Day from SIDS. Only by the grace of God did Latonya navigate her way through depression, suicide attempts and more, to be able to care for her older son.

4 months after the death of her son, she met the man that would later become her husband. They have 2 sons together and 2 grandsons, one from the oldest and 1 from the middle son.

Latonya has a background in Nursing and Science. Latonya is now and has been a Financial Analyst, for the past 18 years, known as The Money Lady. She analyzes and presents budget plans, investment ideas, as well as provide insurance options. Latonya has won many awards

It Is Me...
The Breaking of the Generational Curse

associated with the work she does for her clients, and has been recognized and celebrated as one of the "100 Black Queens of Chicago". She's the Outreach Director of her church as well as an ordained Evangelist, has her own Non-Profit called "Blessings From Heaven". She also helps her 20-year-old son run both of his businesses, Dance Characters and BopKing Larry Entertainment. The 2 of them travel to schools teaching the children about how money works and how they can become business owners themselves. Latonya is a real Comeback Queen with a demonstrated wealth of knowledge of life's hardships, overcoming obstacles, business, wealth creation, and legacy building.

To contact Latonya Willett, you can reach her by email at LatonyaWillett@yahoo.com

It Is Me...
The Breaking of the Generational Curse

The Breaking of My Family's Generational Curse

I thank God for the Holy Spirit. Generational curses are created or made up by having a certain mindset, patterns, behaviors, and decisions. They can be broken through prayer, repentance, and having a made-up mind that you want something different out of life. The definition of insanity is doing the same thing over and over and expecting a different result. If you don't change, nothing else will.

Growing up, I had an aunt and a cousin to stand in the gap for me. My aunt introduced me to God, and my cousin taught me a lot about the word of God. It is because of them; I became a warrior for the Lord. I began to break many generational curses and stand in the gap for others.

It Is Me...
The Breaking of the Generational Curse

As the years went by, I knew that I wanted more out of life. Not just for me, but for others around me as well. I especially wanted more for the boys that were growing up under me. As I looked at the world, I saw that there was a staggering number of African-American boys that, either end up in jail or dead. I also saw that they were not finishing school or getting jobs. I saw how, for the most part, they drop out of school and become the neighborhood dope dealer or user, my family of boys included. I saw, for at least four generations back, young boys and men had never really done anything meaningful with their lives. At that time, my middle son and nephew were small and would account for the next generation. I knew I did not want this for them. I made up my mind that I would try everything in my power to make sure they finished school, not have any children while still in high school, further their education, and either get a job, own a business, or

It Is Me...
The Breaking of the Generational Curse

both.

This is the first step in breaking a generational curse. You must recognize the breakdown, or pattern that leads to this state of being. I could have very well just gone along with the status quo. I could have thought about the scripture in the bible that speaks about the sins of the father being visited upon the child. I could have used that as an excuse to give up on them, but I had a made-up mind, as well as a thirst for the Word of the Lord, that says in *Jeremiah 31:29-34* that He will make a new covenant, and everyone shall die of their own iniquity. You must remember that you are in this world and not of this world. Once you find this out and believe it, it is time to put your faith to work. For faith without works is dead.

This will lead you to the next step, which is facing the situation and dealing with it. You can deal with your curse

It Is Me...
The Breaking of the Generational Curse

in many ways. You can speak life where there is either physical, mental, emotional, or spiritual death. I began to speak life over them. I began to talk about how they were going to graduate from college. I also talked to them about graduating from college. I asked them what they wanted to do once they grew up. My sister and I got them into church again. This time we kept them there. I would do surprise inspections of their phones and back packs. I wanted to make sure there wasn't anyone bullying them, mistreating them or vice versa. I also wanted to know if they were doing well in school. I did not want them to think they would be able to hide bad grades from us. If I saw bad grades, I would talk to them about it and let them know I was there to help. We would go over the homework repeatedly until they were able to grasp it. School was especially important to me, and I wanted them to see that it should be important to them as well. I continued to pray for

It Is Me...
The Breaking of the Generational Curse

them day and night. All the warring and works done in the natural means nothing if you do not understand,

Ephesians 6:12 - For we wrestle not against flesh and blood, but against principalities, against powers, against the rulers of the darkness of this world, against spiritual wickedness in high places.

I continued to love on them, speak life over them and to them. I continued to impart the knowledge of God into them, as well as keep them aware of the power they hold. I also wanted them to know that they were not alone. I noticed a lot of people failed because they did not understand the power they possessed as well and just not having a strong support system. I did not want them to become a statistic before they even had a chance to live. Part of the process was being honest with them. Too often, out of fear, parents will want something for their children and try to push them in that direction without explaining to

It Is Me...
The Breaking of the Generational Curse

them the reasons for their actions and how it will benefit them in the long run. When you are not honest with children, they know it. They will begin to rebel, which is part of what they do to a certain extent anyway. Being dishonest and not allowing them to be part of the process, not teaching them the consequences of their actions, behavior, and decisions will only set them up to fail. This will cause them to rebel on another level and open the door for the enemy to creep in and have his way. That is the exact opposite of what you want to happen.

As the years went by, I introduced them to new things. I wanted them to know there was a world out there bigger than the block in which they grew up. I wanted them to be comfortable traveling the world. My mother was afraid of planes and only traveled on an airplane two times that I could remember. She would let it be known too. I did not want them to be afraid of anything and most importantly, I

It Is Me...
The Breaking of the Generational Curse

wanted them to have the courage to explore the world. I began to take them to Orlando, Florida to Disney World. I also wanted my nephew to go out of town for college. I wanted him to have the experience of being on his own and discovering that he can handle things on his own, but still know that we are there if he needs us. Being out of state would give him more of a sense of independence. It is a way of testing the waters of being a grownup and exercising problem-solving skills. It turned out to be the best thing for him because he aced it! He now has a double Bachelor's degree in Sociology and African-American Studies. He is a Human Resource Business Manager Specialist. He is also, the youngest on the executive administration team for the school where he works.

As for my son, he went to college for a couple of semesters and found that it wasn't really for him. He wanted to dance and expand the business he created at the age of 16. As a

It Is Me...
The Breaking of the Generational Curse

little boy, he would tell me he wanted to be a lawyer when he grew up. Then, one day, he told me he wanted to be a dancer. I really didn't believe him because he always said he wanted to be a lawyer. Until I began to see that he was serious about being a dancer, it was then that I became serious about helping him to accomplish that dream by any means necessary. One day he was at his cousins' house for a baby's birthday party, and they hired entertainment. The owner of the company saw how good he was at dancing, that she offered him a job at her company.

This is a good example of always being of great character and doing something good, because you never know who's watching you. Larry got the idea of wanting to dance because he saw his older brother dance all the time. Well, his older brother danced all the time because he saw me dancing all the time. Also, as Larry was growing up, he never saw me work for anyone. I've always been self-

It Is Me...
The Breaking of the Generational Curse

employed. This gave him the entrepreneurial spirit. He would always watch me interact with potential clients everywhere we would go. He would then watch me as I would break down their personal financial track. He saw how I could set my own hours. There were days when we had appointments back-to-back and wouldn't come in the house until midnight after being out early in the morning. There were other times when I would be able to have fun with the family because I made my own schedule, just as well as other times when we had to let the family have fun because we had to work and fulfill other obligations. So, he is no stranger to hard work. Being an entrepreneur does not mean you just get to do what you want to do when you want to do it. There is much sacrifice so that you can ultimately have the life you want to have later.

After a big misunderstanding with the owner of the company that hired him, she never called him back to work,

It Is Me...
The Breaking of the Generational Curse

and she never paid him for the last two times he worked for her. He was so sad after that. He moped around the house as if someone had died. I told him it was no big deal, and that he didn't need to work right now anyway while in school. It was the dancing that he missed. One day, I asked him if this was what he really wanted to do, and he said, "Yes." I asked him multiple times and the answer stayed the same. That is when I kicked into gear. I asked him what was a character that all the children liked because that would be the first character, I would buy to start his business. Instead of letting the situation take him over and defeat him, it birthed his company, Dance Characters. While all of this was going on, a man who owned a business that dealt with impersonations came to the school to ask his friend if he knew anyone that was a good dancer and a good kid. They referred Larry. This began his next venture. His father and I met with the man and went to the

It Is Me...
The Breaking of the Generational Curse

rehearsals to make sure everything was above board, and he has been with the company ever since that day. All these things happened to him at the age of 16. He later would find favor with the After School Matters staff. He would always participate on the After School Matters dance team. They saw how exceptionally good he was and began allowing him to teach and choreograph some of the dances they would perform. One day, the owner of a wedding band approached his dance teacher and asked her if she knew someone who could dance well with a good attitude; she referred Larry. He has been with the wedding band, and the entertainment company ever since then. Even during the pandemic when there could only be a certain number of people in a crowd, he was able to do impersonations, such as Bobby Brown, James Brown and more. He has even been able to entertain the children for their birthday parties with the cartoon characters and as himself, dancing and

It Is Me...
The Breaking of the Generational Curse

turning the party up. He continues to receive rave reviews for his entertainment and character.

I thank God for all that He has done. I was only the vessel He chose to use. This is nothing and nobody but God moving in our lives to be able to stand in the gap for the next generation to not only break but destroy the generational curses that once plagued our family. He broke the addiction curse, He broke the poverty curse, He broke the literacy curse, He broke the imprisonment curse, He broke the fornication curse, He broke the childhood pregnancy curse, He took away the stagnated mindset and so much more! Thank you, God! Hallelujah Jesus!

Do not be afraid to stand in the gap and break the generational curse that plagues your family. Someone is counting on you. Their life depends on it. Remember, His word says, in *Ezekiel 22:30 And I sought for a man among them, that should make up the hedge, and stand in the gap*

It Is Me...
The Breaking of the Generational Curse

before me for the land, that I should not destroy it, but I found none. And,

Matthew 18:18 Verily I say unto you, Whatsoever ye shall bind on earth shall be bound in heaven: and whatsoever ye shall loose on earth shall be loosed in heaven.

Pray to God, get a made-up mind to stand in the hedge and begin binding and loosing for your next generation, now!

It Is Me...
The Breaking of the Generational Curse

It Is Me...
The Breaking of the Generational Curse

It Is Me...
The Breaking of the Generational Curse

Conclusion

Thank you for taking the time to read "It Is ME... The Breaking of The Generational Curse"

In this anthology, we the Authors, wanted to share our story of breaking the generational curse. Trauma, childhood pain, loving yourself, hurt, heartache, all of it is part of the *"Curse"*. Remember you can stop the curse.

The bible says in **Galatians 3:13-14** ESV / 97 Christ redeemed us from the curse of the law by becoming a curse for us—for it is written, "Cursed is everyone who is hanged on a tree"— so that in Christ Jesus the blessing of Abraham might come to the Gentiles, so that we might receive the promised Spirit through faith.

Remember that your prayers are being heard. You have to continue to love on you, continue to heal and grow into yourself, continue to have faith in knowing that God is working with and for you to end this curse in you and on you. This Generational Curse Stops With YOU!!!

Thank you!

Invisible Daughter LLC

Under the umbrella of Mikkita Moore LLC

www.mikkitamoore.com

It Is Me...
The Breaking of the Generational Curse

It Is Me...
The Breaking of the Generational Curse

Take your time.... Read each chapter as many times as you want.... Then take some time and write your BROKEN Generational Curse....

We are Breaking the CURSE... The CURSE STOPS with YOU....

_____

_____

_____

_____

_____

_____

_____

_____

_____

_____

It Is Me...
The Breaking of the Generational Curse

It Is Me...
The Breaking of the Generational Curse

_____

_____

_____

_____

_____

_____

_____

_____

_____

_____

_____

_____

_____

_____

It Is Me...
The Breaking of the Generational Curse

It Is Me...
The Breaking of the Generational Curse

It Is Me...
The Breaking of the Generational Curse

It Is Me...
The Breaking of the Generational Curse

It Is Me...
The Breaking of the Generational Curse

It Is Me...
The Breaking of the Generational Curse

It Is Me...
The Breaking of the Generational Curse

It Is Me...
The Breaking of the Generational Curse

It Is Me...
The Breaking of the Generational Curse

www.ingramcontent.com/pod-product-compliance
Lightning Source LLC
Chambersburg PA
CBHW071217090426
42736CB00014B/2869